"Highly recommend for anyone wanting to recharge their family gatherings or just wanting to become more thankful for the events in their lives.

'The Thanksgiving Handbook' makes you stop and think about the importance of tradition not just for traditions' sake. It gives you tangible ideas to take a holiday that can become mundane and routine and turn it into a meaningful gathering.

It's a book that anyone could use as a tool to find more meaning and thankfulness in everyday events."

—Leigh Martinka,
homemaker and mother of two children

"I was told about The Thanksgiving Handbook and decided to see if maybe it had some ideas on how to make our Thanksgiving more meaningful. As I read it I discovered what was missing from our gathering together. The author presented simple ideas on how to make the giving of thanks the center of our holiday. I highly recommend it, especially to families with children. The kids loved to be involved with what is suggested in the book."

—Heather Jones, mother of two
Mt. Vernon, WA

"I love this little book with a big message. We can never be thankful enough for the blessings of family, friends, and the many things all around us. This book will give you some fresh ideas and motivate you to make all the holidays even more delightful. I have purchased several copies, as they make great gifts!"

—Mary Ellen Bouren
Phoenix, AZ

"I have enjoyed reading Robert's art-form of "The Thanksgiving Handbook." It brought to me a new challenge that daily gratitude is an adventure with connecting to our Creator. I found important keys that uncover fresh perspective that reveal our loving Father God's intentions towards us. And finally, it gave me tools on how to better connect with His image inside of each of us. I can wholeheartedly recommend it!"

—Debra Comella
Madison, Wisconsin

THE Thanksgiving HANDBOOK

THE Thanksgiving HANDBOOK

Learning To Walk In The Life-Changing Power
Of Giving Thanks

ROBERT COZBY

ReadersMagnet, LLC

The Thanksgiving Handbook
Copyright © 2020 by Robert Cozby

Published in the United States of America
ISBN Paperback: 978-1-950947-80-5
ISBN eBook: 978-1-950947-81-2

All rights reserved. No part of this publication may be reproduced, stored in a retrieval system or transmitted in any way by any means, electronic, mechanical, photocopy, recording or otherwise without the prior permission of the author except as provided by USA copyright law.

The opinions expressed by the author are not necessarily those of ReadersMagnet, LLC.

ReadersMagnet, LLC
10620 Treena Street, Suite 370 | San Diego, California, 92131 USA
1.619.354.2643 | www.readersmagnet.com

Book design copyright © 2020 by ReadersMagnet, LLC. All rights reserved.
Cover design by Ericka Obando
Interior design by Shemaryl Tampus

Acknowledgements

The creation of a book starts with an idea and a blank piece of paper. The next phase requires passion, discipline and a considerable amount of time alone. Then comes discouragement, doubt and writers' block. That is when the value of a support team comes into play to keep you focused on completing the project. For me, it starts with my lovely wife, JoAnn. She understood the need for me to retreat to my mountain artifacts room to get the proper words on paper. I also had the support of my four kids who knew what I was up to and freely gave me supportive words. I am truly grateful to Karly Jones for the beautiful cover photo taken at Butte Peak trail Mt. Baker Wilderness area, WA.

The next big step is finding a trustworthy publisher who shares your desire to get the book into the hands of the intended audience. The team at ReadersMagnet actually found me and convinced me they could take my words and bring all the pieces together and present a beautiful book to the world. Leading the team was Mae Castle, whom I got to know through conversations over the phone each week. Her words were always positive and encouraging, alleviating any doubts I might be having. So, to all of my support team along the way, I give you my heartfelt thanks.

Contents

Introduction 13
    Defines the word *thanksgiving* and gives a
    preview of the three parts

PART ONE: Celebrating Thanksgiving 15
    Discussion of the present-day holiday and suggestions on how to
    make it more meaningful for each family

An Empty Vessel 16
    Details a typical Thanksgiving Day experience for the majority of
    Americans

History 20
    Lays out the historical origins and family traditions of
    Thanksgiving Day

Establishing Meaning 22
    Views the potential depth of meaning
    that the holiday holds for us

A Day of No Thanks 24
    To show the value of saying thank you, we construct a day of no
    thanks

No Right, No Wrong 26
    Establishes the idea of there being another way
    to celebrate the day

Going Deeper, Reaching Higher 28
    Explores the fact that giving thanks has many potential layers

Getting Started 30

Bring a Dish and Bring a Memory 32
    Introduces the idea and manner of involving all who gather to
    give thanks

A Scaffold 34
    Lays out a sample of suggestions for invigorating the day with
    meaning

The Pivotal Moment 36
    Describes the key moment for us as we take
    the day to another level

The Missing Ingredient 39
    Discusses the character quality that the host
    and hostess must exhibit

Luck or Blessing? 41

PART TWO: *One Day at a Time* 43
    Lays out the principle of daily thanksgiving and the benefits of
    becoming a thankful person as it pertains to our relationship to
    God and to those around us

The Party Hangover 44
    Speaks to the challenge of taking our desire to give thanks into
    the everyday

Walking It Out 45
    Gives encouragement to those who have
    the heart to walk it out daily

Tracking Our Life 47
    Using our Thankful Moments Journal to track growth in our
    giving of thanks

From Whence Cometh It Forth 49
    Consideration of the Origin of all of our gifts and what our
    response should be

Gathering Pebbles 51
    Focuses on the value of remembering the moments of blessing in our lives

How Much and How Come? 54

Praise from the Dungeon 56

The Sacrifice of Giving Thanks 57
    Understanding the effort it takes to truly be a thankful person in His eyes

What Are the Odds? 59
    The amazing story of Jesus and the ten lepers is explored and made personal

Latent Power Within 62

Deliverance from Me, Myself, and I 63
    Dissecting and understanding the enemy and forming a battle plan

PART THREE: and Beyond 67
    Explores the value of thankfulness in this life as it pertains to our life beyond the constraints of time and the priceless value of thanksgiving as a gift to God

A Priceless Desert Stone 71
    An allegorical story that brings home the true value of our giving of thanks

The Seven Gifts from the Lips from Beyond 74

From Trailhead to Alpine Meadows 77

Stories of Thanksgiving 79
    Stories of people in everyday situations who have found reason to be thankful

Pebbles Along My Path 90
    A collection of personal thankful moments taken from my own path of life

Thankful Moments Journal 98
    Pages that are laid out as a journal, ready to record
    the moments of thankfulness for the reader throughout the year

References 100

Introduction

Thanksgiving: "To exhibit an attitude of thanks, of gratitude, toward the giver of a gift."

The Thanksgiving Handbook explores the concept, the attitude, and the action of our giving of thanks, both during our designated holiday of Thanksgiving and in our everyday life, with the purpose of expanding the parameters of our understanding as it pertains to our offering up thanks for our blessings, our gifts, and for life itself.

In part one, we will look at the history of Thanksgiving and the foundation laid for our day of celebration. We will look at the beauty and the blessing of the day and discuss ways to bring deeper meaning to what we do on that day, sharing thoughts and stories of people who have found reasons to be thankful.

Part two looks at the development of an attitude of thanksgiving as it pertains to our everyday lives and the potential power it contains to change our lives in a manner that we all desire. We will then build a bridge of understanding between the acquired daily walk of Thanksgiving and the day we set aside to celebrate our year of living and walking.

In part three, our discussion will center on the beyond of this life and the deep and lasting value of our having learned how to be a thankful person while walking our given and unique path here on earth. It will speak to our faith and vision of what lies beyond our physical sight, and it will be a personal journey for you to take as you consider the incentive treasure awaiting you as your thankful heart becomes a shining gift to be presented to the Giver of all gifts.

I will use myself as an example in all three parts that you may identify with my desires, knowledge, and feelings... or not. It will be entirely up to you to tie the parts together in a manner that gives meaning and hope to you in your life.

May the Author of all life have His way with our hearts and minds as we explore a very meaningful and important aspect of our life here on Earth.

Let the journey begin...

PART ONE
CELEBRATING THANKSGIVING

An Empty Vessel

In order to give thanks, one must first recognize that a gift has been given. All of life is a gift, whether we recognize it or not. Every aspect and facet of life has come from something other than our own doing. We are incapable of sustaining or creating life of any kind on our own. The degree to which we recognize and accept this fact determines the potential level to which we will rise in our giving of thanks.

The words *thank you* are spoken or written by millions of people every day. It is an important part of our social language and structure to express and to receive thanks as we work and live together in this amazing country on this awesome planet.

These two words have the power to lift a heart or, if omitted, can infuriate a soul. We as a people are dependent on each other's abilities, gifts, and services in the building and sustaining of our lives and our livelihood. As we communicate with people through the course of our days, we impact lives by the words that we speak.

> A wholesome tongue is a tree of life.
> —Proverbs 15:4

> Death and life are in the power of the tongue.
> —Proverbs 18:21

In America, we have set aside a special day for all individuals and families to celebrate the bounty of our country and the freedom to enjoy it. There is much tradition involved in this celebration, from the type of meal we set out, to the clothes we wear, to who it is we share the meal and day with. We call it *Thanksgiving*.

Yet, in so many instances, the day and the traditions have become empty of meaning and long-term value. Many do not even partake of the act of giving thanks before they devour the spread of food before them, eager to return to the second half of the game or to get the kitchen clean and the leftovers put away. And then it is over, to be repeated again the next year with even less meaning or value. It is the law of diminishing returns. Sadly, some now look forward to the day after Thanksgiving for the sales even more than the day itself.

An example from my own life follows.

It was a few years ago as friends and family gathered in typical fashion for a day of fellowship and food. Gender groups were gathered in their time-worn sections of the house; the men were near the television and snack table while the women were coming and going through the kitchen doors and checking on the kids who were upstairs sharing secrets, or were outside playing basketball in the driveway.

The hum of activity and conversation was in full swing when the three-word announcement "Okay, it's ready!" caused a thundering of feet from all quarters as twenty people gathered around the dining room table. It was a familiar and enjoyable moment as a hungry group of beloved people prepared for a serious moment of thanks before partaking of the diverse spread of food laid out before us.

As was customary, a person was asked to lead us all in a prayer of thanks before we sat down. This year it was my turn, causing a bit of pre-prayer nervousness on my part. Everyone was silent as I asked if anyone had something to be thankful for this year. The quiet became deafening as nineteen pairs of eyes looked down at their plates, hoping I wouldn't call on any of them to speak. I let the quiet continue until an outspoken aunt shared that she was grateful for the health of her family. Someone said they were thankful for their children while another spoke of being glad they lived in a free country.

Then a loud whisper from the hostess declared, "The food is getting cold!" The nervous quiet was broken as we took hands, and I offered up a thirty-second prayer of thanks to God for His goodness, the food, and for each other. Everyone said *amen*, and we took our seats to enjoy a wonderful meal together.

Conversation was dominated with requests for passing this and that and saying how good everything looked and smelled. It was a good feeling to be with all of these people and to be sharing this food and this day. The routine of it all was comforting, but something was missing. I wasn't sure what it was, but then while chewing on a piece of turkey and some mashed potatoes, a thought began to form in my mind, born from my own frustration with the holiday and mixed with my desire for it to become a truly meaningful and honorable feast unto the One who gives us life and all good things. It was clear to me that the parameters of our thankfulness needed to be expanded to include more than just what we could recall at the moment around the table. We needed to come prepared to share, and I suddenly saw how that could be achieved.

We, as a nation, went to the effort to set aside a whole day out of the year to be reminded of our many blessings, so why not come up with a way to bring our blessings throughout the year into the celebration? To offer up a few obvious thoughts without any mention of the personal moments of the year seems almost an insult to the Author of those blessings. It would be similar to dining out at a fine restaurant, being served with great service, and then leaving a fifty-cent tip for the server. They would probably prefer that you didn't leave one at all; at least then they would think that maybe you just forgot.

Our western, secular culture has many positive aspects to it, but one of the regrettable things we tend to do is to take meaningful days and events and turn them into empty shells of their former selves. Part of the problem is our own human nature. We are all comfortable to go with the flow of an event or day instead of interjecting a thought or insight that we might have to make it more meaningful, not understanding that it takes effort to combat two natural and very real laws of nature: incrementalism and diminishing returns. Unless we make an effort to keep the holiday meaningful, it will become meaningless.

One of the potential beauties of Thanksgiving is the fact that everyone, regardless of religious affiliation, can celebrate it. It is a day to be grateful for who we are and where we are; to take stock of what we have in this life and to take a moment to appreciate it.

It is not the purpose of this book to criticize the ways in which we celebrate our holiday; rather, it is my aim to offer suggestions on how to make Thanksgiving more meaningful for all individuals and their families.

History

There are two paths of history to pursue here; we will go down the one for a bit, and then we will come back to the junction and look at the other.

The first path leads us to look at the historical origins of Thanksgiving Day, which is celebrated by both the United States and Canada.

In New England, Thanksgiving was a harvest festival lasting several days with the purpose of thanking God for a plentiful harvest. It was therefore celebrated in the fall, and it still is today. Around the world and for thousands of years, harvest festivals have taken place in order to honor the Giver of life.

In America, the first Thanksgiving was observed on December 4, 1619, and was entirely religious in nature with no feasting. Thirty-eight English settlers gathered along the James River in Virginia to give thanks and then wrote into their charter that a day would be set aside annually as a day of thanksgiving to God.

Over the next 300 years, the calendar date for Thanksgiving would change, but it would always be observed in some parts of the country. In 1863, President Lincoln proclaimed the last Thursday in November as the national day of Thanksgiving. Then, in 1939, President Roosevelt moved it up one week earlier with the purpose of helping businesses gain another week of Christmas shopping. Finally, in 1941, Congress ruled that the fourth Thursday in November would be observed as Thanksgiving Day, and that it would also become a legal federal holiday. So there you have the historical foundation for the national observance of the day.

The second historical path we will look at is the individual family traditions history, established by each family as the way in which they have always celebrated Thanksgiving. These traditions have been observed and passed on to each generation, and rarely do they vary. It may involve the time of day the meal is served, the type of stuffing in the turkey, whether the football games are allowed to be on or not, whose home it will be at, who will be saying grace, whether the dessert is served with the meal or later, whether the guests bring food, or if the host/hostess provide it all.

Now, before you discount these as trivial traditions, let me ask you a question: when was the last time you tried to change one of them? If you had the courage to try, were you successful? I mean, just try changing the stuffing recipe or the potato salad and you will think you have suggested changing the flavor of Coke! We know how *that* went over. Or suggest that maybe, instead of grandma's house every year, we could all come to Uncle Bill and Aunt Sue's house next year.

People like to keep things the same; it gives them a sense of tradition. They know what to expect; it is comfortable. But, there is a downside to the familiar.

A well-known saying goes, "Familiarity breeds contempt." When we become too familiar with the routines and characteristics of a person, a job, or in this case, a holiday, we cease to see and appreciate the beauty and the blessing. We begin to feel contempt for the situation. We go through the routine of the holiday without contemplating how superb it is to have a day set aside for reflecting on the multitude of blessings we were given the past year. The day becomes a time to eat too much and be with family and friends. You may be asking, "What's wrong with that?" The answer is, "Not a thing." Except that you can do all of that at any time, and the name of the holiday is *Thanksgiving*.

So, what do we do? Do we keep the status quo or do we consider injecting a few new ingredients into the mix? *The Thanksgiving Handbook* has some ideas for you to ponder that can enrich and deepen your Thanksgiving holiday experience.

Establishing Meaning

I believe the purpose of the holiday is two-fold: (1) to recognize the traditions begun by the early settlers of this country in the giving of thanks to their Maker for safe passage and for getting them through their first year in a new and unknown country, and (2) to help establish a modern tradition of giving thanks to our Maker in recognition of the multitude of blessings that this free country has to offer us as a people.

From that declaration has come a variety of expressions in the way in which we celebrate the day. We will explore some of those at a later point. The beauty of the day is in the freedom that we have to spend it and express our thanks in the manner we wish. This freedom was bought and paid for by the blood and sacrifice of those before us. It should be on our annual list of things to be thankful for. We have no one telling us how we should spend the holiday. This handbook supports that freedom and offers simple suggestions on how to make the day as meaningful as it can be for the families and individuals who seek to make it a meaningful holiday.

Since I just used the word *meaningful* twice, let's look at the word. It signifies something that is full of meaning to those involved. Therefore, the question should be asked, "What does Thanksgiving and its traditions mean to you?" Is the day full of meaning, or is it just a chance to get three to four days off from work in a row?

Let's think about a few examples, starting with the meat, which is usually a turkey or a ham. In order to have that meat at your meal, something must be killed. In this modern age, we rarely have to personally kill anything in order to eat; it is all done for us and packaged up and ready to put in the oven. Some are even pre-cooked for us. But in the days gone by, someone had to go out to the yard, select a bird or hog, and then butcher and prepare it for the cook. They understood the taking of life so that they could partake and continue to have life. There was a connection to the life given, and they understood it and were grateful.

Other ingredients for the meal, such as potatoes, corn, olives, peas, and carrots are produce and fruit from plants that someone has grown and harvested. If you pick it and prepare it from your own garden, you are more keenly aware of the labor involved in those simple items, portions of your harvest for this year. In biblical days, they would have a two- or three-day harvest feast to celebrate their season of harvest and the year of labor involved. It was meaningful to them. We are now detached from the process and need to be reminded of the labor and the miracle of having food on the table to eat.

Another important part of the tradition involves with whom we share the meal. For some, it is preordained who they eat with or whose house they go to, and they have no choice in the matter. Often, sadly, it is a day we hope goes quickly so we can leave and come home. It is then we are thankful!

Ideally, we are gathered with those whom we love and are comfortable with, the people who have meaning to us in our hearts and minds, people we are thankful for as they labored to help prepare the meal and make the day a memorable one.

I have heard of the tradition of some who invite a person or family of lesser means to their table, who might otherwise not be a part of a Thanksgiving meal and celebration. I see that as a fine and courageous thing to do, adding significant meaning to the day.

As you can see thus far, when we have understanding of the basics involved in the day, we have the scenario for a meaningful day. But there is an element that is often missing from the celebration that can render the day as just another day. That element will be discussed in the chapter "The Missing Ingredient."

A Day of No Thanks

Probably the best way to see and understand something is by viewing the opposite object or quality. For instance, think of how great the morning light is after a night of darkness; or a cool drink of water after a long day on the trail with a dry canteen. I once drank from a muddy pool of seeping water high in the mountains and only remember how good it tasted because it was the only water for miles. If someone has treated you poorly, you deeply appreciate an act of kindness or giving.

So, let's create a day of no thanks so we can see what happens when thanksgiving is not a part of our daily lives.

It is Bill and Sue's anniversary, so Bill decides to get up early so he can make Sue some toast and her favorite jam with coffee. He takes it in and puts it on the nightstand and then takes his shower to get ready for work. Afterward, while dressing, he sees that Sue has had her toast and coffee. She says good morning and happy anniversary, but not a word about her breakfast. Oh, well, maybe she just forgot.

Bill discovers he is now running behind his normal schedule as he hits the main street that leads to the freeway entrance. Of course, cars are backed up and he inches along. As he moves forward, he notices a truck trying to pull out of a side street to get into his lane. He makes the decision to let the truck pull out in front of him, and as he does, a young lady pulls her compact out and squeezes in too. He has to keep from hitting her and notices that she does not acknowledge his act of charity. A few choice words form in his mind as he settles in for a long commute with a bad mood.

Arriving at his office parking lot, Bill hustles to the main door, and as he opens it, he sees Tom hustling along with a box under each arm. He holds the door open and waits for him to come through. He says hello, but no "Hey, thanks." Bill thinks, *Okay, fine,* as he heads to the elevator. As he nears the open door, he sees a group of people already inside. He shouts out for them to hold the door, but no one does. It shuts, and now he waits for it to come back down. His mood is getting darker.

Finally, arriving at his office, he passes Carol, the receptionist, and asks if she could bring him a cup of coffee when she gets a chance. A few minutes later, she brings him a cup as he settles in behind his desk. She waits for a thank you, but because of his mood, he doesn't even look up. She leaves his office and shuts the door a bit harder than necessary. At this, he glances at the door and wonders what her problem is.

Carol sits back down at her desk with a scowl on her face and mutters about her thankless job and wondering what Bill's problem is today. "He can get his own coffee from now on," she whispers.

And so it goes, each person is affecting the next with his or her unexpected behavior of not acknowledging acts of kindness with a simple *thank you.* The need to be thanked for deeds of kindness and the giving of gifts is in our DNA. Greeting card manufacturers have a whole line of cards dedicated to this aspect of human nature. They know that saying thank you is a part of everyday life in every culture in every country.

Is there any aspect of our social behavior that can create a shadow of discord between individuals faster than the lack of thanks? It can cause a stranger to form an opinion of you faster than the speed of sound. Do you want a quick example?

After a fine meal at a notable restaurant, you hand your server, a very friendly stranger, a sizeable tip. They accept it, put it in their pocket, and walk away with no acknowledgment. Now, what is your immediate opinion of that person? It just plummeted, didn't it? You will most likely want a different server next time. Is that decision justified? Probably not, but that is human nature. Those two words can be critical to a good relationship, both in and out of business.

No Right, No Wrong

One of the beauties of Thanksgiving is that everyone can celebrate it, no matter what their beliefs might be. It is not a religious holiday; rather, it is a day set aside for all peoples to gather and to remember their blessings and to be with family and friends to honor the traditions that have been established by that particular group of individuals.

There is no right or wrong way to celebrate Thanksgiving. There is a wide spectrum of traditional activities that are carried out. For some, it is a day of playing flag football, followed by a hot shower, followed by a game or two on the television, followed by a well-prepared spread of food and a glass of fine wine. For others, it is a day of preparing and serving food at a homeless shelter or senior citizen center, followed by a meal prepared at home and a walk through town as the Christmas decorations begin to spring up on Main Street.

Some folks use the holiday as a four-day weekend to drive to the mountains to ski or to visit with family out of town. Many will use a catering service to have a hot meal brought to their home as they lounge about and enjoy a well-deserved break from their work. The list of diverse ways to spend the day is long and they are all good.

So far, I have mentioned the outward expression of our celebrating. There is, or should be, a corresponding inward celebration as well. It, too, is as varied as the individuals gathered. A person can be an atheist or an agnostic, a wondering child or a deeply committed person of long-held beliefs, and we can still gather around the same table and share our heartfelt thanks and

thoughts. It is an all-inclusive holiday and one that holds a place in the hearts of millions of people.

The Thanksgiving Handbook was written with the belief that every heart is capable of growth in knowledge and understanding of the significance of giving thanks. When you couple knowledge with courage to change, you have the makings of a vibrant holiday that retains meaning and expands in its purpose.

With human nature being what it is, we know that people, given the option, will usually take the easy path: just turn on the TV, get the game on, fix a few dishes and a nice turkey, say, "Come and get it," sit down, and start passing the food and no one will complain. Finish the meal, do the dishes, have dessert, finish the football game, grab your coats, and out you go to your various homes. Another Thanksgiving Day has come and gone without the giving of thanks. It was hardly significant and certainly not memorable.

Going Deeper, Reaching Higher

Beneath and beyond each character quality that the Creator seeks to build within our hearts is a deeper aspect, another region if you will. It is the place where He dwells, composed of the qualities that make Him who He is. It is where He would have us be so that we can fellowship with His heart to the degree that brings joy to Him. In fact, let's look at the quality called joy so you can see the degrees of which I speak.

There is a term called *harvest joy*, which describes the joy we feel when the crops are in, the silo is full, and the season of hard labor is behind us. "They rejoice before Thee according to the joy in harvest" (Isaiah 9:3). In our culture, we could think of Friday nights as a form of harvest joy and celebration at the end of the work week, a payday, and a chance to gather with friends for a time of kicking back and looking forward to the weekend. Harvest joy can be intense and full of emotion, but alas, it is short-lived. The next morning comes, the next workweek starts, the ground needing to be made ready for the next season.

Next, there is *paternal* or *maternal joy*, as when we are in the company of our children, family members, or friends. "Live joyfully with the wife whom thou lovest" (Ecclesiastes 9:9). It is a joy related to like-mindedness and kinship, warm feelings, and memories built through experiences together. It is a good joy, and it is longer lasting and foundational to healthy relationships.

And then, there is the joy that needs no external stimulation, for it is based on a deep knowledge of truth and is born within our spirit. It is the joy that is called *unspeakable*, or *inexpressible*, in

human words. "In Whom… ye rejoice with joy unspeakable and full of glory" (1 Peter 1:8). It is the joy that can be our companion as we walk our daily path with the inherent highs and lows. It is a joy that springs from knowledge, and it cannot be diminished. This is the joy He possesses and wishes to build in us.

So when we speak of giving thanks, we can know there are various levels of being thankful, and we can know God wishes to take us to the deepest level of our gratitude for all of life and the variety of gifts we receive each day. It is a path and it is not too steep to get there. But each path has a starting point, and for some it can be the annual celebration of Thanksgiving Day, acknowledging the blessings of the year and the health of family and friends. This handbook seeks to take your hand and nudge you onto the path that leads you to the next level of giving thanks to the One who gives us all things. Encourage your heart with the sure knowledge that He desires for you and your loved ones to one day "Enter into His gates with thanksgiving, and into His courts with praise…" (Psalm 100:4)

Getting Started

To have a fine Thanksgiving Day meal requires forethought, planning, and cooperative labor among those who are doing the cooking. There is the size and selection of the turkey to consider, the type of dressing, the variety of side dishes, and of course, the desserts and who is bringing what.

The time of day for the meal is considered in light of who is coming and from how far away. There's the table settings, the serving dishes, and the wine glasses; there are bedrooms to clean for overnight guests, cars moved for extra parking, and for some, there is a flag football game to participate in and a pro game to watch on television later in the day.

You notice that it is not called *Feast Day*, or *Family Gathering Day*, or *Thursday off Work to Watch Football and Eat Day*. It is called *Thanksgiving*, a day set aside to remember all that we have and to give thanks. To do so in a gathering requires forethought, planning, and cooperation among those who are gathered. This part of the day deserves as much effort as the planning for the meal. For without our giving of thanks, it becomes just another day to gather with family and friends, an obligatory day to observe before we go shopping on *Friday Sale Day* or gear up for *Opening of Skiing Day*. Let's see what we can do to help make it a memorable day for all who have gone to the trouble to gather together and to give thanks.

After the food is set on the table and the guests are seated is when most folks get nervous, most notably the host and hostess. With a diversity of people at the table, they get worried they will make someone uncomfortable with the giving of thanks, no matter

how they handle it. Should they just go ahead and offer a simple prayer, or should they ask if someone would like to pray? Should they remind everyone that the food is hot and just go ahead and dig in, or what?

In most cases, the guests probably expect a prayer of some kind and will welcome it, as long as they are not called on to give the prayer. And, most likely, there will be some who would like to say something about the past year and what they are thankful for.

So what is the best approach for handling this important part of the holiday? Remember, the food is getting cold! And remember, there is no one right way of doing things. What I offer are simple suggestions, a guideline from which you are free to deviate and make your own approach to this important part of the day, this important day of the year.

Bring a Dish and Bring a Memory

Every new way of doing something must be eased into. People, by nature, resist change, even when it is for the better. So, as you read this handbook and find you are excited to make the holiday more meaningful for all, realize that it must first start with you, the host and hostess. Recall some key moments from the present year that cause your heart to beat with thanksgiving. Write them down on a couple of index cards and be prepared to share them at the table with your family and friends.

Are you nervous? Think of it as bringing a dish to the meal. You know that *you* like it, but you're not sure that others will. But you bring the dish because you want to bless other people. It is the same with bringing a memory, a moment when you were blessed or kept safe or were healed, etc. People will love it, just as they do your food.

The next step is inviting those you want to share the day with, either by phone and/or by written invitation. To receive an invitation in the mail denotes something special, an event to be a part of. It helps to set the mental framework for a good and meaningful time together. The following is a sample invitation for you to use as a guide for your own.

You can make it as fancy or plain as you like.

> On Thursday, November ___, we will be celebrating Thanksgiving at our home, and we invite you and your family to be a part of our day.

As a family, we suggest that you bring four things:

1. A thankful heart.
2. A memory from this year to share at the table (you can write it down).
3. A dish or dessert for the meal (let us know what you are bringing).
4. A financial gift to be collected and shared with the less fortunate.

As we celebrate this day of thanks and giving, we look forward to the prospect of having you share it with us.

We hope you can join us…

As the sample invitation suggests, the reason for the holiday is the giving of thanks among family and friends. When people read their invitation, they will begin to think about the items they should bring and will most likely be intrigued by the foundation of purpose that you propose in your invitation to spend the day with you and your family.

Of course, you can just call everyone, as most people do. But people will forget what it was they were supposed to bring, so I strongly suggest that you make or purchase some simple note cards to send out, even to close family members. They will keep the card and use it as a reminder of what to bring. If you believe in the changes we are trying to bring to this holiday, it will be worth your time and money to help make sure that everyone gets the information and comes ready to be a part of the day.

A Scaffold

A scaffold is a temporary structure to give you a place to stand as you work on your chosen project. What I suggest here is like a scaffold, some ideas to help give you confidence and direction for your sharing time.

Keep the pre-meal activities and traditions the same. If watching football before the meal is part of your day, then watch it and enjoy the freedom to do so.

The preparing of the meal and the setting of the table should be done as you always have. Ask for volunteers to help with it so they can be a part of the effort to make a fine-looking table of bounty.

Set a bowl on a table close to the entrance to the dining room with a note designating it as the bowl of collection for the less fortunate. Place your donation of cash in it before people arrive so they can see what it is for. (More on this later.)

As the people gather at the table for the meal, have them be seated and get comfortable. Since great effort went into the timing of the dishes being done and being hot, let this be the time for a simple prayer of thanks offered by the host or hostess. Some folks like to join hands at this point, which is a fine thing to do. Before the prayer, and while you have everyone's attention, let them know that they will gather again at the table before or during dessert time to share their memories and discuss the past year. This is a good spot to let them know where the charity bowl is if they would like to participate. Tell them it is going to the local homeless shelter or wherever you have decided.

After the meal is finished, hand out "Thankful Moments" cards with pencils. Tell them to write down at least one moment or event from the past year that they are thankful for. Remind them that you will gather at the table later for dessert and sharing. Even the kids can get involved; they love these kinds of activities.

Some folks like to clear the table and take a break before dessert, and some like to clear the table and have it right away. As the host, you can pretty much decide how you want to do that by getting a consensus from your guests. Either way, this is a good time to relax and share together. There are no hot dishes to concern anyone, and everybody has had their food needs met so they can sit with a cup of coffee or tea and listen to what you, the host/hostess, have to share.

It is important that all are gathered and not spread out in the kitchen and television room. You may have to make an effort to have them come to the table again, even if they do not want dessert. If the kids want to play in the other room or outside, you may want to let that happen. But kids tend to love being a part of these kinds of activities and love to hear stories. Take the lead on this and they will be happy to follow.

The Pivotal Moment

You are the one that has read the handbook, and *you* are the one that has decided to try and bring a sense of meaning and purpose to the gathering. So it is *you* that now shares with these people you love about how the meaning of thanksgiving has changed for you.

At this point, to help you along, you may want to actually show them the handbook and read a portion from it that has spoken to your heart and mind. Trust your audience; they love you. Trust me when I tell you that what you are doing could change a life, and what you are sharing will strike a cord of understanding and truth in their hearts. If this sounds a bit melodramatic, permit me to remind you that we are looking to "celebrate Thanksgiving, one day at a time," for the rest of our lives and beyond. We are not just trying to spice up a holiday. We are trying to help people be thankful for who they are and what they have on an everyday basis. Remember that each and every person on this earth has an intuitive knowledge that everything in their life has come from the Source of all things. To some, it is a mystical force, while to others it is the father God of all life. At this moment, it matters not what the people at your table believe as it pertains to God. It only matters that you believe each person at your table wants to be a thankful person.

Okay, so you have everyone back at the table eating their dessert and wondering what you have in mind. So, tell them! Speak from the heart and make it personal, telling them of your desire to not just have a fine meal with friends, but to truly celebrate in the giving of thanks for this past year and the moments contained within it.

Share with them the moments that have impacted your life and that you are thankful for. Show them how you recorded these moments throughout the year in the back of your handbook. If you feel that a verse of Scripture would be appropriate with your group, share with them from 1 Chronicles 16:8, "Give thanks unto the Lord... and make known His deeds among the people."

When we speak of His deeds before people and give witness to the moments we have recorded in our memory and on paper, it strengthens our faith and our powers of observation as daily blessings come our way. Take out your note cards and share with them the moments you remember and are thankful for: the sunset at the beach with your mate... the healing of your dog after being hit by a car... your promotion at work... the day you smelled sweet peas and cried out of pleasure... the day you visited a friend in the hospital and came away with a renewed sense of thankfulness for your health... the near-accident on the freeway back in July... the storm in October when the power went out and you built a fire in the woodstove, listened to the sounds of the fire, and appreciated the pleasure of being warm on a cold day... the day back in August when your lost wallet was found with everything in it... and so forth.

Now, encourage them to share something with the rest of the group and see how it goes. You may need to gently prod, but maybe not. If you have a relaxed atmosphere, people generally like to share their stories. And everyone has a story. Things happen to everybody; we just don't always remember it. But if we do and then we share it with someone, it sticks with us for a long time. As we recall the event or the moment, the emotions are revisited—be it fear, anger, joy, awe, whatever it was—we remember it, and we are thankful all over again.

As they listen to you, they will most likely remember at least one moment that they can share with the rest. Some may have come with a thought written down, but the chances are that it won't happen until the next year, when they know what to expect. There may be one or two that are inspired to know about the handbook and where to get it. Show them yours and point out the Thankful

Moments Journal in the back. They can use any small notebook if they want to begin recording moments right away. In fact, an excellent method is to start a Thankful Moments Journal on your computer. If you spend a lot of time on one, it is very handy for you to click over to your journal and record something that inspired thanksgiving in your heart. You can then print up the chosen moments to bring to your next Thanksgiving gathering.

After the time of sharing and discussion, you may want to take a moment and offer a collective prayer of thanks, or you may not, depending on the type of group gathered. If you do, there may be a person who would like to offer it after recalling a special moment from the past year.

The key point to remember is that nothing has to be forced; you are just friends gathered together discussing life during this past year. Look around the table and ponder that one of them could have been killed this year. They weren't; they are all here. But Life is precarious and shouldn't be taken for granted. Tell them what you just thought of and how thankful you are that everyone is still with you on this amazing earth. I am sure they will agree with you! This is easy stuff, as long as you have the courage to get it started and to speak from the heart.

The Missing Ingredient

Earlier in the handbook, I mentioned that there is an important element or ingredient that can make this day memorable and fresh. Without it, you will have just another holiday gathering.

My Grandma used to make superb breads and pastries, and she told me of the time she mixed up all the ingredients for a large batch of bread and put it in a bowl to rise so she could cut the dough into loaves to be baked. Well, she waited and waited, but the dough did not rise. She put her hand on it and smelled it. The dough was not spongy and full of life. All the ingredients were in there, except she had forgotten to put in the yeast! All of the waiting in the world would not have helped those ingredients to be turned into bread. We both had a good laugh about that one.

Every Thanksgiving, we have the ingredients for a memorable day, but there is often no life or growth to it. It needs yeast; it needs you and me to have the courage to offer a new element to the day, a way to incorporate the events of the year into a celebratory day.

God looks for ways to insert yeast (courageous people) into bowls of dough. He knows that the law of life will cause it to grow and become beneficial to all who partake of the bread. He has placed you in this group of people to be the yeast that causes growth in their understanding of thankfulness and of life.

The first time we do anything is usually the hardest. Try standing up on a surfboard for the first time, or on a pair of snow skis. That's right... down you go. Do you quit? I don't think so, not if you want to get good at it. Your mind and body must learn the nuances of the new activity. It would be easier to just sit in the snow or splash in the water, but that's not much fun compared to skiing and surfing.

Having a collective share time around the table is new for everybody. Please remember: we are all programmed to eat the meal and then go back to the game or chat in the kitchen or whatever else we usually do after the meal. And no, there is nothing wrong with those activities. We simply desire to make room for another aspect to the day, an aspect that can in fact change the day and change our year ahead.

Take heart and have fun as you share the things you see and learn along your given path of life.

Luck or Blessing?

Since you will most likely have a mixed group of people at your gathering, the likelihood of all having a common faith is slim. Therefore, I would like to prepare you for a topic that will most likely come up and one that you need not fear. In fact, it can make for healthy and interesting conversation, of which you should have no apprehension.

It has to do with the question of whether our moments that we share are a result of being blessed by a God who loves us, or if they are simply a matter of dumb luck—you know, being in the right place at the right time and all? The resulting conversations are valuable because by getting people to speak on the subject, it helps them to see what their viewpoint on life really is. There is no need to argue the luck versus blessing topic. Healthy discussion? Sure. That can be fun. But no one should be ridiculed for his or her viewpoint; rather, they should be applauded for their courage to share.

Again, the beauty of Thanksgiving is that all people can celebrate it from their heart because being thankful is a heart response, not a religious one. You can be a devout atheist and still be thankful for your life and the things you have and the moments you share. It is an attitude, not a theology; a manner of living life, not of defining it.

You can travel to any country, visit any village or isolated tribe of people, and you will find thankfulness in the hearts of its citizens. And, without fail, you will discover that a depth of thankfulness will be in companion with humility and sincere graciousness. It works its way through our entire system of attitudes and character qualities. That is why it is referred to 140 times in the Bible and why God speaks of it as such a valuable quality. It has the power to change us because the action of saying "I thank you" declares that you did something for me that I recognize as being a gift from you. This requires humility, which is, by the way, a universally admired quality.

PART TWO
ONE DAY AT A TIME

The Party Hangover

Well, here we are; the annual Thanksgiving party is over. We ate too much, we sat around too much, we were with certain people too much, and now it's the weekend and there are sales and shopping to do and... hold it! We need to stop right here.

We have some things to discuss, so put your feet up, grab a cup of something hot—or cold—and let's talk.

When I spoke with you in part one about Thanksgiving Day, I told you that it had the potential to change your life; that it was about more than just spicing up a holiday. If it did achieve that to any degree, then I am glad. But it is only the beginning. A better holiday experience probably won't change your life, but a new daily walk has that capacity.

Every path has a beginning, and part one was the beginning, the trailhead. We hung out with friends, we ate and drank, we maybe went skiing, and we maybe thought about the many blessings in our life, had a prayer of thanks, and then called it a day. That's good. But now it is the day after, so to speak, and it is time to hit the trail if we want to ascend and get a better view of things.

We now know that the attitude of giving thanks was never meant to be observed on just one day out of the year. That is our feast day, our public gathering and sharing day. We now have to adjust our thinking and incorporate a new attitude into our daily walk. This is where the power lies and where I collect my pebbles of thankful moments for the feast day next year. This is where I begin to truly see life as a giant gift that is given to me in daily moments.

Walking It Out

First step, first lesson: put your finger at this page, close the book, and close your eyes. Now, take a deep breath of air and let it out. That, my friend, was a gift given to you. Now, say *thank you*. To whom, you ask? That is up to you, according to your faith and understanding. I know to whom I say it, and hopefully you do, too. The important thing for right now is that you realize that air is a gift, without which we would become as dust. I know you know you need it, but have you ever given thanks for it? If you haven't, but you did it now, you are walking a new path, a path that ascends and will lead you to life beyond what you presently know.

Now, for the sake of example, turn to the back of the handbook to the part called "Thankful Moments Journal." On page one, write down the date and then record the fact that on this day you gave thanks for the air that keeps you alive. Add any thoughts or insights you might have on the subject, and now you have a note to bring (if you choose) to the next Thanksgiving! How about that? Not so hard. And because you wrote it down and expressed an attitude of thanks for air, you will notice how much more aware you are of the simple gift of breathing.

I had a close friend who passed away from emphysema. Toward the end of her life, she would have given away her whole doll collection just to take one deep and satisfying breath. I would visit her and almost feel guilty because I could breathe normally and she couldn't. On a good day, she could get half of a deep breath. So, be thankful for your air and the ability to take it in. Remember: on the day you quit breathing, you won't need to anymore.

Since you are reading this book, I could probably do a mini-profile on you and be fairly accurate. Let's give it a shot: (a) you dislike pretense and meaningless holidays. (b) You want to be a better person and become more aware of life and people around you. (c) Your understanding of God is less than you want it to be. (d) You are a thoughtful person and are basically glad to be alive.

Did any of the arrows hit the mark? Not hard to do, actually. The point of the exercise is to show you that you were already on this path before you picked up the handbook; you have already been thinking about these things. Which is perfect because then what you discover here will become what's called "a word in season" for you, meaning that you are hearing it at the moment you are ready to implement it. You've experienced it before: like when you are in a class or in a church service where it felt like the teacher was talking just to you, deep in your heart. Or, the opposite: you are bored with the dry words and can't wait to leave. Then months or years later, you recall something said and you are moved by it and take it to heart. The apple is ready to be picked, as they say. It is in season.

When Jesus walked the earth, He would frequently say, "He that has ears to hear, let him hear." (Luke 8:8) He knew that unless people were ready to take His words to heart, they would be like sand in the mouth. You can't spit it out fast enough. So, if you are ready, let's keep walking and maybe pick up a pebble or two along the way.

Tracking Our Life

In ancient times, people who loved God and believed that all of life was a gift would record moments of His care and miraculous works on behalf of them by building stone altars or memorials to remember it by. (Please take a moment and read the account of Joshua and his people building a memorial to a miracle in Joshua 4:1–9.)

Then, let's say they are out for a hike with their family, and they come upon a pile of stones. They would stop and tell their children a story about the day God did a certain caring deed for them on that spot. Sometimes they would carve it in a tree or engrave it on a stone slab. It was their way of remembering, of tracking God's care for them throughout their life.

That is what this is about: tracking His care and love for us as we walk our given and unique path in life, and the metamorphosis that is taking place within us as we walk it out.

One person who was exceptional at tracking his life was King David, the author of most of the psalms. He spoke of his beginning, how even within the womb God was forming him and caring for him. "For You created my inmost being; you knit me together in my mother's womb" Psalm 139:13.

He recalled his teenage years and deeds done, of becoming a man and watching God lead him in battles and giving him victory. He also spoke of his missteps, his errors, and the loving forgiveness he was shown. He concludes with where he is headed and the joy of being ushered into the presence of the One who gave him life.

David was not afraid to look within his own heart. He was courageous in his walk and dutiful in his recording of the gift of life. He exhibited the three qualities we need to walk this path: honesty, courage, and humility. I must honestly look at my life, have the courage to declare the truth, and the humility to know from where it has come.

You can use the Thankful Moments Journal, your computer, or a notebook of your own to write things down for your own review or for sharing with others, like on Thanksgiving Day. Recording our moments of insight, blessing, miraculous care, tragedy survived, joy, pain, victory, or defeat is our way of tracking and building a foundation to sustain us when we feel most alone or depressed.

Thus far, I have connected the dots of our giving thanks with the knowledge of a loving God from whom all things come. So let's say that your life experience indicates that there may not be a loving God, and that your good moments and blessings are simply a result of careful living and happenstance. Or maybe you are a believer in good karma due to your giving of yourself. Does that change the value of developing an attitude and life of giving thanks? No, but it *will* limit the depth of it because there is no persona in the Giver. The value and power of being a thankful person does not rest on our theology or the lack thereof. Recognizing our blessings does not change the object of our worship. *We* are the ones that are changed, and not only us, but also those with whom we relate. Remember the "day of no thanks" and how it impacted so many? It also works conversely. When I display humility and graciousness in all that comes my way, I positively impact those around me. My belief or disbelief in a loving God does not distract from my need to grow in character qualities. But to know there is a persona behind the Author of the gifts will enlarge the parameters of how deep my thanks can grow. The following story illustrates this point.

From Whence Cometh It Forth

So, imagine it is your birthday, and about twenty people are invited, and they all show up bearing gifts and an appetite for food and fun. You share the food and all have a good time. Someone brings out the cake and candles; they all sing while you blow them out, and then you move to the gift table.

You open them one at a time—the card first of course—and thank each person for their gift. The mound of gifts gets down to one, and someone hands it to you. You look and notice that there is no card. "Who's this from?" you ask. The guests look around, expecting someone to speak up. No one does. They all help look for the card under the table, in the hallway, where the coats are hanging; but no card.

Someone shouts out, "Open it. Maybe it's inside." So you carefully open it, and still no card. The gift turns out to be a rare book that you had been saving money to buy; a book that you thought only you knew about. You are overwhelmed at the value of the gift and the fact that it is in your hands.

"Who do you think gave it to you?" someone asks. "I have no idea who would have known about the book," you say.

"So, how are you going to find out who it is?"

"I don't know; maybe they'll call me or something.

But I *will* find out."

Not knowing would bug you, wouldn't it? If someone knew you well enough to give you a gift of value anonymously, you would give your best effort to discover who it was so you could thank him or her. Because it is a person, your quest is personal. If it had been a generic book with a card on it that stated it was from a large, faceless corporation that randomly sent gifts out to individuals on their birthday, you probably would not feel the need to take your search any further. You would have said, "Hmm, that was nice," and that would have been the extent of your thanks.

So we can see that if we believe that the source of our gifts is a nameless, faceless, gaseous power somewhere, we can still feel thankful, but it will not be personal; it will lack depth.

When the veil is lifted enough for you to see that there is a persona behind it all, your search will begin in earnest, and it will not be in vain. Your giving of thanks will then have the capacity to bring tears to your eyes.

Gathering Pebbles

A number of years ago, I was into mountain climbing in a serious way. It was a passion that consumed my time and energy, both on and off the mountain. I would expend great effort to reach a summit, enjoy the moment, and then begin pondering the next trip. But before I made my way down from the summit, I would pick up a stone and put it in my pack. There was often a weatherproof box on the summit with a notebook and pencil for people to sign and date as a record of their climb. I rarely did this, because my memory stone was sufficient for my records. I kept them in a box at home and would pull them out, look at them, and recall the climb and the view from the summit. One of my favorites was a stone that I gathered near the summit of Mount St. Helens before it was blown to smithereens in 1980.

People collect a number of items as they travel as a way of remembering their trips. The list includes lapel pins, beer steins, miniature flags, hats, t-shirts, and of course, picture postcards. There is a difference between collecting items for their value and collecting items as a means of remembering.

As for myself, I enlarged my collecting to include any memorable trips to the beach or various wilderness areas. I once discovered an abandoned beaver pond on a hike and brought home a piece of beaver-chewed wood. Kids like to gather shiny stones and pieces of shell from the beach. I think they like them mostly for their beauty, not necessarily as a memory reminder. But I know some that do.

One of our weaknesses as humans is that we tend to forget important things. I am sure that women would agree that men are

the worst when it comes to remembering things. They are probably accurate in that observation. I think I was told there have been studies done about that, but I can't remember for sure.

In the book of Timothy, Paul encouraged his protégé, Timothy, to stir up the memory of people of faith about all that God had done for them and the future home He had prepared for them. When people get depressed or suicidal, people who love them try to get them to remember all that they have to live for in order to get them out of their downcast mood. People who have been married a long time tend to forget the beauty and love of the person they married. Anniversaries are meant to remind them of those things. Our culture has made it an occasion for gift buying. It should also be for remembering.

Your Thankful Moments Journal is your jar of pebbles to go through and remember the past year and the memorable moments that came your way. It is first and foremost for your benefit, to lift your spirit and to keep you focused on the fact that your life is unique, that it has value, that it has purpose, and that someone cares for you.

As you go through your jar of memories, certain moments will stand out. If you will transfer these onto index cards, you can then bring them to your Thanksgiving gathering to share with the group. Now, you may not think they are that memorable, but let me assure you that the smallest incident or event can be of great value to someone listening.

I can remember one time when a lady shared the moment she was in her garden and smelled something wonderful and followed the smell to her sweet pea flowers. She picked one and held it to her nose and remembered playing in her Grandma's yard and seeing her smell her sweet peas. She teared up at the memory, and did so again as she was sharing with us. She wasn't the only one. Her sharing reminded me of when I was a young lad in Fairbanks, Alaska. My mother couldn't grow many things because of the poor soil, but she did get some pansies to do well, and I remembered picking one and really looking at the beauty contained in that one flower. It stuck with me, and I have loved pansies ever since. They are a memory stone for me. All of that came from a simple sharing of a small moment in a lady's garden.

Parents will tell you that some of their favorite memories of their children were small moments in themselves: a look of wonder as they showed them the stars for the first time; their first fish caught; their daughter in her first dress; trying to blow out candles with chocolate cake in their eyes; looking at the many critters in a tidal pool; listening to the laughter coming from their room during a slumber party; and the list goes on.

No moment is too small if it has significance in your memory. There will be the near-tragic accidents, the healings, the promotions, the births; all of the big things to share. It is all of value and yet so easily forgotten. That is why in the first section of this handbook I mentioned my dismay that we limit our prayer of thanks to the obvious blessings of that day. There is so much more that can be offered up in our sacrifice of thanksgiving. And it is quite a bit of fun to sit and listen to people as they share and relive their significant moments of the past year.

How Much and How Come?

The success of any endeavor is defined by what the goal of the endeavor is. In sports, the goal is to win the game. In the process of playing the game, each individual player tries to do his or her part in a perfect manner. Perfection is their individual goal within the larger team goal. For instance, if you are shooting free throws in a basketball game, you will be trying to make every one of your shots. It is rarely accomplished, but that is your goal. You want to make all of your shots in order to win the game.

Now, when it comes to the matter of walking our path with a thankful heart, what should be our goal? What mark should we aim for? Well, let's see what the Master has to say about the subject.

> Sing and make music in your heart to the Lord, always giving thanks to God the Father for everything.
> —Ephesians 5:20

> Do not be anxious about anything, but in everything, by prayer and petition, with thanksgiving, present your requests to God.
> —Philemon 4:6

Everything? Yes, everything. That is God's goal that He sets for us in this arena, so that is what we should aim for. Again, it is like being at the free throw line and the coach saying that we should have the goal of making every shot. By having that as your goal, your shooting will improve because your focus will be sharper.

Now, what if I say that I will give you 100 dollars for every shot you make? Will that help to sharpen your focus? I think so. We will call it *treasure incentive*. Some players have incentive clauses written into their contracts. For us, it is the vision of having the treasure of a thankful heart to set down at the scarred feet of our Master as we are led through the gates and into the court of His presence. "Enter into His gates with thanksgiving and into His courts with praise; be thankful unto Him, and bless His Name" (Psalm 100:4).

When Jesus was here on earth in human form, he had a purpose and a focus to His life that was like a laser beam. His choices and decisions were made based on what His goal was. And what was his goal? To be obedient to His Father's wishes and to free a captive people and present them to the Father. That was His treasure incentive as He lived His life and suffered and died a cruel death. He had hope and vision as His path took a bloody turn, a vision of us being presented as a treasure. We have Him to thank for our life because He kept His focus and fulfilled His mission and purpose as he walked the path His Father had given Him.

Our walk in this life is incentive based, too: to build a thankful heart as a treasure to be presented to the One who made it possible for us to have a life in the realm of beyond. If we keep our focus, we can walk through anything, even our times of suffering. How? By remembering, "All things work together for good to them that love God, to them who are the called according to *His* purpose" (Romans 8:28 KJV)

Praise from the Dungeon

There is a recorded story of Paul being imprisoned for telling people about the gift of life that Jesus brought to all men. He was beaten and then thrown into a dark cell. He was hungry, sore, cold, and probably wondering why God had not kept this from happening to him. The prison guards were used to hearing moaning, crying, and complaining from the prisoners and had probably learned to turn a deaf ear to it all. But tonight, a different sound was coming from the depths of one cell. It was the unmistakable sound of a man singing. Not a song to break the monotony of his situation; rather, it was a song of praise and thanksgiving.

I can see the guard quietly making his way down to the cell to confirm what he thought he was hearing, wondering if maybe the prisoner had lost his mind and had forgotten where he was. Instead, he sees Paul with arms raised and tears in his eyes as he sings of his God's glory and power to deliver him from the hands of the enemy. His circumstances gave him no reason to be thankful; yet, his faith-filled heart was bursting with praise because of his intimate knowledge of God and His hand over all situations.

All things are good and all things have a purpose for us as we remember our treasure incentive. To be thankful is not a wasted exercise. There is a present and a future reason for our efforts. Let's keep a laser focus as we move forward on our path to Him and into the beyond.

The Sacrifice of Giving Thanks

> Let them give thanks to the Lord for His unfailing love and His wonderful deeds for men. Let them sacrifice thank offerings and tell of His works with songs of joy.
> —Psalm 107:21–22

Does the term *sacrifice of thanksgiving* seem strange to you? I mean, how hard can it be to say thank you? Why does God call it a sacrifice? Let's explore along this path for a bit.

There is a common expression that is used these days: "Thank God." Actors in movies use it a lot in dramatic scenes where maybe something bad was expected to happen and it doesn't, so they exclaim, "Thank God." You also see it used by people being interviewed in the news after an accident or a type of natural disaster. The reporter will ask, "So you lost your home in the tornado. Did everyone get out in time?" The victim then responds, "Yes, thank God."

So, is there anything wrong with saying that? Well, no, but it is an excellent example to help point out the difference between having the thought that thanks should be rightfully offered to God and actually doing it.

Here is another example that is related to the topic. A news anchor is relating the story of a famous person that has been injured and is interviewing one of the family members. At the conclusion of the interview, the anchor says, "Our thoughts and prayers go out to you and your family." Now, that is a nice thought, but unless the prayers are actually offered, that is all they are; just thoughts.

This is not to put down the good thoughts; rather, it is to point out the difference between thinking a good thought and doing something. It is the doing that requires sacrifice of time and effort, and therein lies its value.

All of us are very good at thinking of good things to say and do. For instance, you haven't seen one of your friends for quite some time, and then you happen to see them at the mall and start to chat. Within ten seconds you will surely utter those famous, hollow words, "Hey, man, I've been meaning to give you a call!" Or, "Hey, I thought about you last week and meant to call and see how you're doing!" Then, depending on the level of your friendship, the wisecrack comeback goes, "Well, it's the thought that counts!" But does it count?

A friend has just said that he thought about you but did not take the time to contact you.

Now, why am I probing this aspect of human nature? To show how weak we usually are when it comes to following through on good thoughts and intentions. We all understand and share this weakness and usually cut each other a lot of slack. The real problem, though, is when we transfer that acceptance of good intentions over to our relationship with the One who made us.

Let's just say, for example, that you haven't spoken to God for a while, and then let's just say that you are walking in the park with your dog, and there on a park bench is God. You're not sure how, but you know it is Him, and he invites you over to sit next to Him. He, of course, doesn't look at all like you had pictured Him! But, that's another story. Now, be honest; as you look Him in the eye, do you figure that you will utter the words, "Hey, I thought about you last week and meant to talk to You!" I think we would realize in a split second that our words would sound quite empty.

It is the acting out of our thoughts that brings a smile to His face and to His heart. It would be a wonderful moment if we could hear Him say, "I enjoyed you sharing your thoughts with me last week when I came to your mind. It warms My heart to hear from you."

It is the same with people; when we actually hear from someone who has been thinking of us, it warms our heart and makes us feel that we mean something to them.

What Are the Odds?

When good things happen to you this coming year, what are the odds that you will stop what you are doing and offer a moment of thanks? Will you think about it? We know now that it starts with a thought, a good intention. But will action follow the intention? What odds do you give yourself? Would you say one in twenty; one in fifty?

Let me tell you a story, an ancient story; one that is as true today as it was when it took place nearly 2,000 years ago. It is recorded in the best-selling book of all time, the book that speaks to the heart of every matter, every characteristic of the human heart, and every experience. It speaks truth to all who seek to understand and to grow.

It is recorded in Luke, chapter 17:11–17:

> Now, on his way to Jerusalem, Jesus was traveling along the border between Samaria and Galilee. As he was going into a village, ten men who had leprosy met him. They stood at a distance and called out in a loud voice, "Jesus, have pity on us!" When he saw them, he said, "Go, show yourselves to the priests." And as they went, they were cleansed.
>
> One of them, when he saw he was healed, came back, praising God in a loud voice. He threw himself at Jesus' feet and thanked him, and he was a Samaritan. Jesus asked, "Were there not ten cleansed? Where are the other nine? Was no one found to return and give praise to God except this foreigner?" Then he said to him, "Rise and go; your faith has made you whole."

Ten men who have a terminal, disfiguring, society–isolating disease have their request for healing granted by a man they have never met, yet who they hear has great power. They obey His simple command, and in the process of walking, they are healed.

Now, imagine yourself walking with nine of your best, disfigured friends, and as you look at each other you see health returning to your bodies. You touch your face and your hands while joy and disbelief begin to flood your brain. From all ten mouths we can imagine words like, "Oh, my God… oh, my God! Oh, thank God! I don't believe this! He did it! It's gone! Oh my God!"

Right? Can you hear yourself saying that? I would, that and a lot more. Good words expressing good thoughts and intentions while they walk away from the source of their healing. But then, one stops and looks back and sees Jesus standing there looking at them. He now has a decision to make: Does he keep walking with his newly cleansed buddies, or does he go back, alone, and give action to his thoughts by saying thank you to the One who made it all possible?

It is the exact same decision we have the opportunity to make every day. In this marvelous story, the odds turn out to be one out of ten; 10 percent sacrificed the time and energy to give voice to their thankful feelings. 10 percent got their eyes off the blessing long enough to look at the blesser. Amazing, isn't it? It says that "they" all called out for help, so you would think that as a group, "they" would all go back to the One who gave them the gift of health again. I would bet that, just like us, they felt that feeling thankful was the same as giving thanks. It is not. The giving requires sacrifice; the feeling does not.

This story also shows us God's viewpoint on our response to his blessings. He asks the question, "Were there not ten cleansed? Where are the other nine?" He expected all ten to come back and say, "Thank you, sir, for your kindness, your mercy, and your power to heal. We are not worthy of your attention, but we thank You."

There is another phrase of truth in the Book that says, "We love Him because He first loved us" (1 John 4:19)

We are built to respond to love; it is in us. That is why we have thoughts of being thankful. It is our heart speaking to us, urging us on to express our thanks for blessings and for love that comes to us each and every day.

When you teach your child to say thank you for a gift given, they never question why they should. It is in them to do it; they just need your guidance to learn how. Just like swimming. The instinct to swim is in every child, every baby. They just have to be taught how to get better at it. If they put if off until they are older, they will have to learn to overcome their fears. Kind of like us learning to give thanks in front of family and friends around the table, huh? It is in us to do it, but we are fearful.

It is time, one and all, to make the sacrifice of thanksgiving and to put down our fear and pride so we can walk with a humble heart in recognition of all that we have been given from the One who thought of us before He placed Orion in the heavens. Let's determine to be the one who stops and comes back to give thanks instead of just walking on our way, thinking about how great it was to be healed.

Latent Power Within

We just finished reading and studying one of the most amazing short stories ever recorded. Why can I say that? Because two short paragraphs encapsulate the human condition and attitude toward God and His attitude back toward us. Give people a bit of blessing, and all they can do is think of themselves. Only one man thought beyond himself. And what set him apart from the others? An attitude of thanksgiving.

I mentioned earlier in the handbook about the power of giving thanks and the potential to change our lives. To understand that power and to demonstrate it, we need to take a few moments and do a word study. Are you ready? Let's do it.

The power that is linked to the attitude and habit of giving thanks is what is called *latent power:* "being present, but not visible; not apparent to the eye; existing as potential; laying dormant."

Latent power is not a sword or a machine gun. It is not huge biceps or strong legs. It is what I would call "Bruce Lee power." As you know, Bruce Lee was a master of martial arts, and yet to look at him in street clothes, you would never know it. He was small, almost skinny, but he had tremendous potential power within him. It was lying dormant until it was needed. It was latent power.

If you were to look him in the eye, you would see it, and if you were smart, you would not mess with him. You would not want to be the stimulus for his response! Latent power is of no value unless there is the will to use it. All ten lepers had the power, but only one used it. The one man got the stimulus to go back and give thanks. His response to the stimulus is what caused him to be blessed by God. It was latent power in action. He overcame the prevailing voice within, the same voice that all of us do battle with. It is the voice of me, myself, and I.

Deliverance from Me, Myself, and I

Welcome to the battlefield, ladies and gentlemen. What is the battle for, you ask? It is the battle for control; control of you and of me as we walk through this life.

But you say, "I *am* in control of my life!" Okay, maybe you are, and maybe you're not. It all depends on how you want to live. Let's take a look and you decide if you are or not. Fair enough? Let's continue.

I am going to propose something to you that is based on one section of Scripture and on my own experience in life. To properly determine whether my proposal is accurate or not, remember the three things that I mentioned earlier that are required for us to grow and understand this latent power of thanksgiving.

They are: courage to look, honesty to evaluate, and humility to accept the results. Armed with those three qualities, we can now proceed.

Every day of our lives, you and I do battle with an invisible enemy, hidden away deep within our nature. We face each day wanting to be the best we can be, but by the end of the day, we realize we lost some battles; we failed. Our words and actions were not all that we wanted them to be. So what's the answer? Well, let's first look at the enemy.

In 2 Timothy 3:1–5, the enemy is exposed and broken down into nineteen pieces for us to look at and ponder. God says that during our present "perilous times," our hearts will be: (1) lovers of ourselves, (2) covetous, (3) boastful, (4) proud, (5) blasphemous, (6) disobedient to parents, (7) unthankful, (8) unholy, (9) without natural affection, (10) promise breakers, (11) slanderous, (12)

lacking self-control, (13) angry, (14) despisers of good people, (15) traitorous, (16) head-strong, (17) high-minded, (18) lovers of pleasure more than lovers of God, (19) religious but denying its power.

Do you recognize any of these? Did you do battle with any today? Did you win?

It is humbling to see myself exposed for what I am inside. But let's not be ashamed, because He already knows who we are. That is why He bled for me and for you, to break the power of the enemy and give us the tools to finally become victorious.

Now, here is my proposal, what I believe:

If we will simply focus on number seven, we can gain a foothold over the other eighteen! If we can become thankful instead of unthankful, we have pulled up the shades on the dark, lurking power of the others. Take them one at a time and think about it. (1) Lovers of ourselves… selfishness. If I have gratitude in my heart and mouth to God for life and who I am, I am already thinking of someone other than me. That is a victory right there!

Covetous… looking at what others have instead of all that I have. My Thankful Moments Journal shows me that I have quite a lot, actually, so I don't need to look at what others have. Another victory!

Boastful… thinking I am really something. As I lay my thanks at His feet, I realize that I am nothing apart from His graciousness.

Pride… believing that I am self-made and that I can do no wrong; I am unbroken and resistant to being changed. To give thanks forces me to lower my head, both literally and figuratively.

Blasphemous… speaking with a foul mouth, cursing, using God's name in a negative manner. As I let forth a stream of thanksgiving (clean water), I am now more aware of my negative words (muddy water), and I seek to clean up my mouth.

Disobedient to parents… rebelling against the care and authority that God has placed in my life. It is very difficult to utter thanks to God for our parents and then turn around and show disrespect for them by being disobedient. Victory again.

Unthankful… receiving my daily gifts of air, clothing, shelter, food, a place of employment, family, friends, and every other item that I have in my possession and not being grateful for them. The obvious remedy is to be aware of the fact that they are gifts and to let the Giver know I am thankful.

Unholy… living in a manner that is unclean in thought, word, and deed. If we would make the effort to give thanks as a daily habit, our inner voice of desire to live clean before Him receives a higher position of being listened to and obeyed as we make our multitude of decisions for living. We begin to abhor our unclean manners and begin to move toward a cleaner lifestyle.

Without natural affection… not feeling a basic, natural love for family, friends, and people that we meet in our daily walk. There is a deadness of spirit, a numbness of heart when it comes to feeling affection and love. Maybe we had a traumatic experience or an abusive childhood. Maybe life has beaten us down and we feel cold inside. If we can muster the courage to offer our thanks for being alive, a warmth will begin to mend our dulled "affection nerve endings." We will begin to feel, to notice others, and to have emotional ties to them once again.

Promise breakers… making promises and commitments to people and to ourselves that we never keep. Being a "man of my word" has lost its meaning. I make promises in the moment but fail to make the effort to bring it to pass. By giving thanks for life, I become aware of my responsibilities when it comes to speaking truth and backing up what I say. I also realize how troubling it is when someone breaks his or her promise to me. I now make the effort to be a person who people can believe in when it comes to doing what I tell them I will do.

Slanderous… using my tongue and heart to defame, belittle, disparage, discredit, disgrace, dishonor, degrade, and humiliate. Slander is a very unattractive use of the gift of speech. My tongue gets me into more trouble and causes more damage than any other part of my body. To be victorious in this area, I must start with the giving of thanks for this gift of being able to communicate with others in some manner. By being thankful, I become more conscious, more aware of how powerful the tongue is and how greatly I need to control it for the good of others. I will see small victories, and I will be encouraged to continue and will give thanks for the victories each day.

Go through the list one at a time and test it for yourself. All nineteen characteristics have to do with me, myself and I. My belief is that a thankful heart will put us on the path to victory over all of them, and my experience proves to me it is true.

So, will having a more meaningful Thanksgiving Day give me this victory? No. Will writing a few things in my Thankful Moments Journal equip me for this fight? No. But it is a start, just like a trailhead is the start of a strenuous climb up into the mountains. The further up the trail I go, the stronger I get. Likewise, the more my heart is opened to all of the beauty and wonder of giving thanks, the more victorious I become in doing battle with that which is an enemy to my growth.

Giving thanks to God is like putting a key in a door; you must turn the key, open the door, and walk through. The walking is your sacrifice; the walking is an act of your will. As the leper turned and walked back to the Master, he was delivered from his selfish ways. He wasn't just healed of leprosy; he was healed of a selfish heart. That was the greater miracle for him and that, potentially, is the greater miracle for us.

And to think that all of this could start by simply sitting around a table with family and friends, discussing the many blessings from the past year. Donning my pack and deciding to start walking up the trail into the mountains high above gains me the glories of the alpine meadows. It is a small beginning with a great reward.

PART THREE
AND BEYOND

This section of the handbook acts as a demarcation line for us. For those with a faith in the reality of a hereafter and a reunion with the loving Author of your life, you will most likely continue your path through this book into part three. For it is in part three that the true value of parts one and two become evident.

For those of you with convictions to the contrary, this may mark the end of your interest. Then again, your curiosity may prompt you to take a peek and either affirm your present position of life or open your heart and mind to the idea of what is presented here for your consideration. I hope it is the latter.

A few decades ago, I was a John Muir disciple. Let me explain.

John Muir was a lover of the natural world and a writer who was able to convey his love of mountains and rivers and glaciers and pure wilderness in a manner that was both eloquent and easily understood. He also loved the Creator of these natural works of art and wove the two loves together into a tapestry of words that could move you to want to see his wilderness and learn about the Creator of the natural world.

I thought of the mountains as my worship center and had no use for man-made churches or their worship services. They made me extremely uncomfortable and did not speak to my heart. I had many friends who went to church, and one in particular was a close friend. He persuaded me to come to a Bible study in his home and promised there would be no pressure put on me to even participate. So, as a friend, I went. I was wary, but curious, especially when the idea of a personal relationship with the Creator of all life was put forth. It seemed to be the piece I was missing.

My excursions into the mountains had been like visiting an art gallery. Now I was being told that I could gain audience with the Artist behind the artwork if I would simply accept His free gift of life, paid for by His death. It spoke to my heart and was devoid of religiosity. It made sense and tied all of the loose ends of life together and gave me a hope of life beyond my climbing days here on this beautiful earth. I accepted the gift and determined to get to know this awesome Artist while I continued to climb His amazing mountains.

Decades later, I still love the mountains, and I am still in love with the Artist responsible for them. He has made some incredible promises to us and gives us every reason to believe He is a man of His word.

One of those promises is that He is preparing a special place for us to live and walk with Him beyond the constraints of time. It is a place where full citizenship is required and can be had while still here on earth. Your name is written into a book, and the ink is the blood of the Son who gave His life for us.

To receive our citizenship, we simply respond to the urgings within to believe the promises made by the One who bled for us and loves our unworthy hearts. Now, that's not too much to ask, is it? Open your heart to His promises and you shall be filled.

Part Three will be explored with the premise that life beyond is a reality. There is enough evidence to sway the most ardent skeptic, but it is not the mission of this book to try to persuade you. If you were sitting down with me in person and had heartfelt questions about the subject, I would be most enthusiastic to rap with you about it. In fact, if you have a desire to correspond with me about life beyond or any aspect of this handbook, there is an address in the back of the book where you can reach me. Be fearless in your pursuit. He knows you well and wants to show you His gifts even more than you want to find them.

For myself, the evidence comes down to two things:

1. I placed my faith in the word of someone who said they would heal me and change my life, and He kept His promise. He then said that there is a beyond, so I believe Him.
2. It makes total sense to me that there would be life beyond, and now, all of life here makes sense. For me, it is now a fact.

In His wisdom, He has chosen to keep a veil over our eyes concerning the details of our future life. We can see it, but, it is fuzzy; the image is blurry.

> For now, we see as through a darkened glass; but then, face to face. For now, I know in part, but then, I shall know even as also I am known.
>
> —1 Corinthians 13:12

I believe it is fuzzy so as to help us stay focused on the details of life here so we can be involved with the cocoon stage of our development in preparation for our emerging as flutterbys, fit to inhabit the land of beyond. (Author's note: the word *flutterby* is not a typo error. I refer to butterflies as *flutterbys* because it best describes the little critter of which we speak. Personally, I think maybe the person who named them made a typo. I mean, when you see one, they flutter by, don't they?)

As we discuss the action, the attitude, and the habit of giving thanks, we see the immediate value of doing so as it impacts our lives and those around us. It first of all gives a depth to our Thanksgiving celebration and is a blessing to those gathered. Then, as I incorporate it into my daily living, the blessing and power becomes magnified as I walk it out and allow other character qualities to follow thanksgiving into my soul. My eyes are now opened to the reality of life on a daily basis, which is to say, I am the recipient of a gracious gift giver every day, and now I confess that I am aware of it and want to thank Him for it. That is part one and two in a paragraph, in a nutshell.

Now, if the value of giving thanks in my life were to end with my death, it would still be of great value for how it enriched my life and those around me when I was alive. So when we come to discover that the value becomes enhanced in our life beyond, it gives even greater credence to the value of said character quality in the now.

Let's build an example to help us see it.

A Priceless Desert Stone

Let's say I am exploring the desert of one of the southwestern states. I am wandering around and trying to absorb the beauty and the silence of this immense desert. I am out at night with a flashlight to maybe see some critters, and as I hold the light to see where to walk, I spot a shiny object in the sand. I pick it up, and it is a clear stone of some kind and looks kind of cool. It is hard to really see it, so I put it in my pack and take it back to camp.

The next morning, after some cowboy coffee and breakfast, I remember the stone and dig it out to see it in the sunlight. It looks even shinier, and my companions think it might be worth something. They encourage me to have it evaluated by an expert. So when I get back home, I take it to a geologist, and he studies it with his practiced eye and tells me that I have found a two-karat diamond. He tells me that, in the rough, it is worth maybe five hundred dollars. But, if I allow it to be cut and polished, the value would be in the thousands. I am understandably shocked. I was looking for critters and serendipitously found a diamond!

I walk back to my car, looking at the stone with a new appreciation. Rubbing the stone, I try to peer into it, past the rough and stained exterior. To me, it already has a beauty, but now I know that with some work and some financial sacrifice, it could become a gem of great value.

My curiosity and sense of responsibility for the stone makes the decision to have it cut and polished easy. I entrust it to a jeweler who sends it out to a gem cutter, and now I wait for him to call.

A month goes by, and then it is ready. I enter his shop and he sets it on the glass display case in a velvet box. The anticipation I feel to see it surprises me. He slowly opens it, and there it is, sparkling in the lights above the display. It is spectacular!

My mouth hangs open as I pick up the diamond and slowly turn it in the light. There is no resemblance to the rough stone I found in the desert. It has been transformed into a stone of great value. As I talk with the jeweler, an idea comes to me. I ask him to set it in a ring that I have seen before in the display case. He agrees it is a good choice, so I leave it with him and head home.

Since I have decided that my girlfriend of three years is the one for me, I want to present her with the diamond ring instead of selling it, telling her the story of discovery and development of this stone. As I drive home, I mentally track the path and value of this diamond. It went from a rough, nice-looking stone in the sand to a gem of high value, to a highly-valued gift for a first class lady. My heart tells me that, for both her and myself, the true value of the diamond will soon become priceless for what it will one day represent to us.

Did you follow the allegorical truth of the story? The stone is our thankfulness as it is discovered in the soil of our earthly heart. It has a beauty to it in its raw form, but the true value is hidden within.

The cutting and polishing by the gem cutter is the process of our incorporating our thankfulness into our daily walk and the revealing of the inner sparkle that it bears.

And how does it become a priceless stone? When we appear before our Master in the beyond realm of our life and present our thankful heart to Him as a humble gift. For us it is an unpolished stone, a meager attempt to give Him something that He cannot buy for Himself. But for Him, it is a priceless gift for what it represents. How awesome is that possibility? Talk about incentive treasure! That is the ultimate.

Earlier I mentioned how the realm of beyond is fuzzy as we seek to peer into it and use our earthly experience to comprehend the realm where our paths are taking us. The book of Revelation,

the last book of the Bible, provides a fertile field for us to wander and wonder at the beauty and the mystery of life during and after the curtain comes down on time. It is the only realm we have ever known and by which we tend to discern the future.

In the book of Revelation, there are types and symbols and allegorical stories and beings of great power and responsibility in the unfolding of this period. We should read this book and try to see and understand what is meant for us and not be put off by what we do not comprehend. We should remember that we are as caterpillars trying to understand the realm of flight. That is a lot to ask of a caterpillar, and yet, He has promised to teach us if we will be sincere in our desire to learn about Him, about ourselves, and about the amazing land of beyond.

The Seven Gifts from the Lips from Beyond

Our path now leads us by faith to look into the future to a place that He has prepared for those who love Him. Although there are many things to explore here, we will focus on that which pertains to our study of thanksgiving and how it relates to our present walk on earth.

As we take the time to peer into this revealing book, the book of Revelation, we see many wonderful aspects and characteristics of the land beyond. One of them, which is welcome to us who were born on this temporary earth, is the fact that it is permanent; it is our eternal home. It is recorded that Abraham "…looked for a city which has foundations, whose builder and maker is God" (Hebrews 11:10)

We all seek some sort of permanence in our lives and in what we build. But the earth is a land of decay and change. Maintenance is required to retain the original condition of objects, be it a home, a car, or a work of art. The masterpieces of art from the past centuries must be reworked to bring back their luster. Our homes and cars succumb to decay and rust. It is all temporary, and we are just passing through on our way to our permanent home in the land of beyond.

> Now these (people of faith) all died in faith, not having yet received the promises, but, having seen them afar off and were persuaded by them, and embraced them, and confessed that they were strangers and pilgrims upon the earth… But

now they desire a better country, that is, a heavenly one; therefore God is not ashamed to be called their God, for He has prepared for them a City.

—Hebrew 11:13, 16

So, what does all of this have to do with thanksgiving? Well, I will tell you, and I will show you.

When we work on things that we know are temporary, we tend to not do our best work. For example, if you are building forms for pouring concrete, you do not worry if the joints are perfect or if you bend a nail or mar the wood. You know it is temporary. But, if I ask you to build a frame for a picture that will hang in a prestigious gallery for the next few centuries, you will give me your finest efforts.

Therefore, if you can believe that developing the habit of giving thanks and having a heart full of thanksgiving has a place of permanent expression in the land of beyond, you will most likely give your best while here on temporary earth as it pertains to developing your daily walk of giving thanks.

Let's take a humble peek into chapter seven of the book of Revelation. Read the whole chapter, but focus on verses 9–12.

> "...A great multitude (of people), which no man could number, of all nations and kindreds and tongues, stood before the Lamb (Jesus), clothed in white robes and with palms in their hands; and they cried out with a loud voice saying, 'Salvation to our God which sitteth upon the throne, and unto the Lamb.' And all the angels stood round about the throne, and the elders and the four beasts, and fell before the throne on their faces and worshipped God, saying, 'Amen; blessing and glory and wisdom and *thanksgiving* and honor and power and might, be unto our God for ever and ever.'"

Seven gifts from the lips of those who are gathered before their Maker, the One who bled and died for them here on earth so they could be with Him in His permanent home, together, forever. And one of those gifts is thanksgiving.

Imagine a million people gathered together; imagine a 100 million. Now, imagine a gathering "which no man could number" and imagine them, with one voice, speaking forth the seven word gifts from their hearts to the heart of their loved One, their God.

Wow, talk about chills down the spine and tears down the cheeks! Imagine it. Here sits God's gift to man, Jesus, and around Him is gathered Jesus' gift to God: us. And what do we have to offer to the occasion? Seven word gifts from our heart to His. And one of them is thanksgiving. Absolutely awesome!

I don't know about you, but I think now is not too early to start getting used to saying thank you to Him for all that comes into my life here on earth. When I one day bow before Him and speak of blessing, glory, wisdom, thanksgiving, honor, power, and might, I would like my heart to be a vessel full of the knowledge of what I am speaking of. I want the thankful moments journal that is being recorded in my heart and mind to be full. How about you?

From Trailhead to Alpine Meadows

There is a particular spot in Mount Jefferson State Park in Oregon that is, for me, a most sanctified place. It is a hidden, rocky knoll, surrounded by mountain pines and hemlocks, sheltered from the wind, and just large enough for a tent and a campfire.

From this knoll, one has a view of the north side of Mount Jefferson that can cause you to forget to breathe. Your eyes take in the crevasse-filled glacier, the rocky spires, and the alpine-covered ridges that lead your vision to the summit where just one person can safely stand at a time. In the middle of the view flows a spectacular waterfall, the sound of which can be heard at night as the wind calms to a quiet whisper through the pines beside your tent.

When the nights are clear and you sleep in your bag outside the tent, the crisp air is your lens to the heavens filled with bright, twinkling stars and the occasional shooter across the sky. The wind in the pines, the thunder of the waterfall, and the crackle of the campfire are your sounds of the night. To try to sleep is the last thing on your mind, but you finally do, and then you are awakened by the red fire of the sun as it crests the eastern ridge. The new day has come, and as you roll onto your stomach and look straight ahead, you see the light of the sunrise chase the shadows from the crevasses and turn the summit pink before the snowy white color returns.

Now, with energy bar and coffee cup in hand, you climb up and sit on the highest rock above the tent and look down the valley toward the northwest. From this vantage point you can see the trailhead meadow in the trees far below, and glimpse sections of the trail as it courses along the ridge to the north and back into the Douglas fir forest. You see from whence you started and then you turn back to the peak to see your destination. It is a wonderful spot, a gift from the Architect of the landscape, to me.

As we come to this place in the handbook, our rocky knoll viewpoint, we gaze back to the trailhead, to our look at Thanksgiving Day. We see how we started and how we meandered up the trail, looking at our daily life, and how we can grow in our habit and understanding of being a person with a thankful heart for all things. We see ourselves getting stronger the farther up the trail we go. Through breaks in the forest, we catch glimpses of the peak beyond and the beauty and challenges that lie ahead.

We are now at this wonderful place where we can view our beginning while we ponder the beauty that is *beyond* and above us. We see the trailhead (Thanksgiving Day), the trail (our daily walk), and the distant summit (the land of beyond), all tied together. The tough parts of our path now seem trivial as we see where it has gotten us and where it is we are seeking to go.

For myself, I am thankful I could take this journey with you as the Author of all life seeks to teach us that our life here on earth has great worth as it relates to our future in the beyond with Him and all of His extraordinary creations, of which, "The eye hath not seen, nor ear has heard, neither has it entered into the heart of Man, the things which God has prepared for them that love Him" (1 Corinthians 2:9).

In other words, it is beyond our imagination to fully know what He has prepared for us in the beyond life. If we should need incentive to grow and become all we can be in this life, that should take care of it. All of our trials here will pale as we "enter into His gates with thanksgiving and into His courts with praise" (Psalm 100:4).

All questions shall then be answered; all hearts shall then be full as we encounter the mesmerizing beauty of His presence and the endless realm of His heavens, designed and built for His pleasure and the joy of those He has chosen to call His own.

Stories of Thanksgiving

There had been a storm along the coast a few days earlier. The major portion of the rain and wind has subsided, but the surf is still thundering onto the rock-strewn beach below the grassy outcropping upon which Sarah is sitting. Her dark brown hair hangs straight and wet against her neck and face. The cold, light rain that drips from her chin is mingled with warm tears of pain and confusion as she watches the surf break into pieces against the jagged rocks. That is how she feels, in pieces.

She knows she is cold because she is shivering, but she doesn't care. The pain in her heart is her main concern, along with her amazement that she has been fooled so easily by her husband of three years. Her friends and family were also fooled after giving their heartfelt support. And her three children seemed to take to him right away. To have a man in the house who appeared to share her beliefs was important to her, and she had high hopes for a new start.

"How could we have been so deceived?" she cries. With that, her face goes into her cold hands as she recalls the hidden addictions that her husband had brought into the marriage. The abuse was mostly mental; fits of anger and being gone with flimsy excuses. The kids were hurt and confused, and that was the hardest part for Sarah, letting them down again by her choices.

With her face still in her hands, Sarah feels warmth on her neck and back. "I must be getting sick," she thinks, as she lifts her face to the horizon. Light hits her full in the face while the ocean below her is still dark and wild. Squinting into the sky, Sarah sees that the clouds above her have parted enough for a single shaft of sunlight to beam down to the outcropping of rock where she has chosen to sit. Her body begins to warm while the storm rages on.

As she pulls her wet hair away from her face, she stares up at the sky, and light begins to penetrate her heart and mind. She feels loved and cared for by the One who sees all and forgives all. Hope begins to fill her heart as she asks to be forgiven for the choices she has made. She thinks of all she still has and thanks Him for her loving kids, family, and friends. Tears of joy mar her vision as she determines to start again, and this time to do it with His guidance and with patience. As she looks out to the incoming waves, two seagulls are just above the curling water riding the cushion of air being forced up. They seem to be in love with just being alive as they twist and dive and rise into the air.

"That will be me," she whispers. "I'm going to enjoy just being alive and being loved by you. If you bring a God-loving man into my life, I will be open to that. But if not, that's okay too."

As Sarah rises from her perch and stretches her numb muscles, she knows she will not forget this scene or the lessons she has learned. Her body is cold, but her heart is warm as she moves forward with confidence and thankfulness.

TJ is staring at the wall of his office, trying hard not to look out his window at the cherry blossoms and the bright March sunshine. It is Monday, and the paperwork on his desk gives him the sick feeling of it being a long day and probably a long week. He wants to be outside, doing anything but what is before him. Being moved from a computer systems installer to an assistant in the marketing department has given him a set schedule and an increase in wages, but it took him from having a flexible schedule and the chance to be outside at least part of the day. He is in a sour mood and knows he shouldn't be, but he doesn't know how to shake it.

At five minutes to ten, he gets up, stretches, and heads toward the break room for some much-needed coffee and hopefully an apple fritter to ease his growling stomach.

Walking down the hall past other offices, he comes to the glassed-in office of Personnel. As he absently glances in, he notices three people sitting in chairs with their resumes in hand, waiting for their interview time. He slows and as he does, one of the interviewees glances up and catches his eye and gives a quick nod before looking back down. TJ nods and resumes his walk toward his apple fritter.

As he pours his coffee and munches on his fritter, he thinks of when he was in that interview room and the emotions he was feeling at the time as he sought to end his long unemployment drought. His savings were drained, and the room was full of what he figured were people more qualified than himself. He remembers the feelings of hope and joy when he was told he could start the following Monday.

As TJ refills his coffee cup and heads back to his office, he feels the dark cloud lift from his mind as he realizes how fortunate and blessed he is to be employed and to be doing something that he at least halfway enjoys. He finds himself giving thanks for his situation and offers a quick prayer for the young man in the waiting room as he bends to the task of clearing his desk of the piles of work before him.

Joey is bothered as he comes through the front door of his home, throws his schoolbag in the corner, rips his jacket off, and throws it into the corner. His mother, Lois, watches from the kitchen and knows something serious has happened to upset her normally-composed thirteen-year-old son.

"Why don't you come and sit here with me, Joey, and tell me what's up?"

"I'm not in the mood to talk, Mom."

"I know, but that's usually when we most need to talk. Come on over, and we'll figure it out, okay?"

Joey comes and sits with her and, with watery eyes, says, "I didn't make the varsity soccer team."

The pain in his heart is evident, and Lois has to fight back her own tears, as she knows how hard he has worked to make the team. She has picked him up and watched him practice numerous times. He is a good athlete but is still growing and is not as coordinated as he will one day be.

"Are you going to quit?"

"I don't know. I feel like it. I'm better than some that made it. I don't understand why I didn't make the team. I hate just being on the practice squad."

Lois prays as she thinks of what to say to her hurting son.

"Joey, you know how good Michael Jordan was at basketball, right?"

"Yes, Mom, everybody knows that. What about it?"

"Well, I bet there's something you and most people don't know about Michael."

Joey stared at his Mom and wondered what she knew about Michael Jordan that he didn't. She stared back at him while he thought about what it might be.

"So, what is it, Mom?"

Lois takes a swallow of her tea, puts the cup down, and says, "Did you know that he got cut from his high school varsity basketball team?"

Shock is evident on Joey's face as he says, "No way!" A smile is on her face as Lois says, "Yup. The coach didn't think he was good enough, so he cut him. I guess he proved him wrong in the end, didn't he? Michael knew he was good enough, and instead of quitting, he decided to work harder and prove it. And the rest, as they say, is history."

Joey shakes his head as he says, "I can't believe the coach was that stupid. How could he do that?"

"Well, we're all human, Joey, and we don't always make the best decisions about ourselves or others. But, if you have God-given desire and talent, and you know it, then you just have to keep working and prove it. Look, you have that and much more. You're healthy, you have friends, you have a good mind, and you have me. Now, do you feel like quitting on us?"

Joey has to smile at his Mom as he says, "No, Mom, I don't feel like quitting."

"Well then, what do you say we stop our yappin' and thank God for what you do have and ask Him to help make you the best you can be, okay?"

"Yeah. All right, Mom."

With that, they take hands and join together in thanks to Him for all that they have and all that is to come their way, both good and bad. And there isn't a dry eye in the room.

Stan and Rob are in a ditch, a very deep ditch. It is their job to be in the ditch, and they love it. They are known among the construction crew as "tunnel rats" because the ditches they work in are deep and as dark as a tunnel.

They are part of the septic line crew, laying four–foot sections of concrete pipe, thereby replacing old lines for the city.

The crew has a good team: the Digger runs the backhoe, which can dig down to twenty feet; the Jackals drop in and pump up hydraulic jacks to support the two sides of the ditch; the Rocker uses a Bobcat loader to drop gravel into the ditch ahead of Stan and Rob to lay the pipe on. They then grade it out with shovels and a level and call for pipe to be dropped down by a topside man. The rubber gaskets are slipped on and the next section is rammed home.

It is tense work, but exciting for the two twenty–year–olds who have worked together for over a year. They are buddies both in and out of the ditch and watch out for each other as they take turns grading the gravel and laying the pipe. They both watch for stress cracks caused by equipment vibrations and poor soil as they wait for the Digger to dig the next section. Minor cave-ins are common and are scooped out as they occur so the work can continue.

On this day, a Tuesday, the crew is planning a tie-in to the mainline, which goes through an intersection with heavy traffic vibration. The backhoe is near the limit of twenty feet and everyone is anxious to finish this line and move on to a shallower ditch.

Stan and Rob are keyed up as they climb down the ladders into the dark ditch. With helmets on their heads and shovels in their hands, they make their way to the end of the pipe to wait for the final section to be dug out. Because of loose soil conditions, traffic is being routed away from the line to minimize the chance of a cave-in.

As the backhoe finds the mainline, a small cave-in occurs, causing the ditch sides to be too far apart for the jacks to support them. The decision is made to scoop out the material and hold the bucket against the weak side while Stan and Rob prep the ditch for gravel. One moves forward while the other watches for soil movement.

Adrenaline is flowing and senses are sharp. Topside conversation is halted as they listen for commands from Stan and Rob. Gravel is shoveled down by hand to minimize vibration. Sections of pipe are dropped and all is ready.

It is Stan's turn to lay the pipe with Rob watching directly behind him. As Stan moves forward to attach the next section, Rob senses that something is about to happen. Instantly, he grabs Stan's belt from behind and yells, "Stan, out, now!" In one fluid motion, he flings Stan back and then beyond himself toward the back of the ditch beneath the jacks. Rob leaps after him with his shovel trailing behind him as fifteen feet of the sidewall breaks loose and crashes into the space just occupied by the tunnel rats. The force of the air knocks both of them flat and covers them with a layer of soil and sand. Then, quick as cats, Stan and Rob make for the ladder and start to climb. It is then that Rob sees that he is holding the last two feet of his shovel handle. Sticking it in his pocket, they both scramble to the surface to be greeted with smiles and back slaps from the relieved crew.

A knowing look passes between the two rats as they stand at the edge of the cave-in to look where they would have been. Stan stares at Rob and has to ask, "How did you know?"

Rob is still pondering the estimated five tons of soil and asphalt in the chasm below. "I don't know how, Stan. I just knew."

"Well, brother rat, I'm sure glad you did. What say we take a much-deserved break?"

"Yeah, brother, I think I could sit for a bit."

Rob never forgot that day as he often ponders how he knew. Instinct? Maybe. A quiet voice? Maybe. He will probably never know. But, ten years later, he still has the shovel handle, and he did discover the name of the One to thank for the miracle that day. He always honors the memory with a quiet prayer of thanks to the One who watches over every sparrow and every moment of His children's lives, especially when they're in a deep, dark, and dusty place.

Sharon is having one of those days when you question the decision you made to have children. It is July, it is lunchtime. Their south-facing home at the end of a lane on the outskirts of Missoula, Montana, is already too warm.

Her three-year-old son, Tommy, is arguing again with his five-year-old sister, Sarah. *What is it this time?* she wonders as she leaves the kitchen to see what the problem is. Both are on the floor in Sarah's room, and both are pulling on the same stuffed animal to gain sole possession.

"Both of you stop, now. Sarah, let Tommy play with his Pooh Bear and you get something else."

"But I had it first. He always gets to play with it."

"Sarah, you're the oldest, so let him have it until after lunch; and tell him you're sorry for fighting over it." Sarah lets go and puts on her best pouty face with no apology forthcoming.

"All right; Tommy, come get your sandwich. Sarah, you'll stay in here until you can come out and apologize. Tommy, tell Sarah you're sorry."

"I'm sorry, Sarah." With that, Sharon takes Tommy's hand and leads him into the kitchen, closing the bedroom door behind her a bit harder than needed. Seating her son at the table with his sandwich and juice, Sharon wishes again that her husband, Andy, was here and not still gone driving his long-haul truck. The kids don't fight as much when he's home.

She is worn down and doesn't want to lose her temper with her kids. She sits with Tommy and eats her sandwich while listening for Sarah to come out. All is quiet while they eat. Sarah has always been stubborn and finds it hard to apologize.

Sharon guesses she got that from her. Even when she knew she was wrong, it was always so hard to say it. She prays that Sarah will break quicker than she did. "I wish I could be a better mother, Lord," she whispered. With that, she fills the dishwasher and starts making a new batch of sun tea when she hears the bedroom door close. Sarah is standing there, red-eyed, with wet cheeks. Sharon's chest hurts as she watches her daughter struggling. She holds out her hand and says, "Come here, Sarah." The gesture is too much for Sarah as she starts to cry and run to her mom, hugging her leg. Sharon hugs her back and holds her against her leg. Finally, with her voice muffled against her mom's leg she says, "I'm sorry, Mom."

With tears making their way down her cheeks, Sharon looks upward and very quietly says, "Thank you, Father. Thank you for these two children and the love I have for them. Help me be the best mom I can be for them. I love you…"

Kneeling down, Sharon and Sarah hug. Then, looking her in the eye, Sharon says, "Let's get you that sandwich."

Patrick is, as usual, late for his appointment with the architect that is presenting the final blueprints for the office building to be built by the company Patrick works for. As supervisor of new construction, he must follow the project from blueprint to completion.

This Monday morning the sidewalk down Seventh Street is exceptionally busy with people who seem to have all the time in the world. Trying not to be rude, Patrick navigates through the crowd as best he can with the hope of getting three blocks down to the architect's office in ten minutes.

A clear path opens along the edge of the building all the way to the next crosswalk. Patrick dashes down the open path and gets

nearly to the corner, ready to cross the street, when all of a sudden, down he goes. Landing on his shoulder and hip, he rolls to a sitting position to assess the damage and discover why he went down. Rubbing his sore shoulder, Patrick finds himself looking into the face of a homeless man that had been reclining against the wall of the building. He is rubbing the shin that Patrick had tripped over in his haste to make the crosswalk light. As Patrick moves out of the way of the pedestrians and grabs his briefcase, he offers an apology to the man and asks if he is okay. When he says he is, Patrick realizes that he knows this man, a vendor for a supply company he used a few years back.

"Is your name Roger?" he asks.

"Yeah, how do you know me?"

"I'm Patrick. You used to come into my office as one of my suppliers. What happened to you?"

Looking down and pausing, Roger says, "My drinking got the best of me. I got laid off, and my wife asked me to leave." He spoke for another two minutes, and as he did, Patrick noticed the pint of bourbon in his right hand. Looking back into Roger's eyes, Patrick felt a stab of pain in his heart as he thought of Roger's fall from success and of his own after-hours social drinking. He realizes that this could be him.

Reaching into his jacket pocket, Patrick says, "Roger, I have to get going, but I want you to take this card and call me. I know of a company that could use you and your experience. So call me, all right? And here's some money for the phone call. I'll be expecting to hear from you." Roger takes the card but hands back the money. "I'll call," he says and extends his hand to Patrick in thanks.

Grabbing his briefcase and dusting himself off, Patrick makes his way to the corner and waits patiently for the light. He knows he is now late and doesn't care. He can't stop thinking of his encounter with Roger and hopes that he does call him.

The light changes and, as he crosses the street, Patrick quietly gives thanks for his brief encounter with Roger and vows to help him if he can. The thought of making an adjustment to his after-work routine also crosses his mind.

Andrea quietly shuts the examination room door and makes her way down the hallway to the receptionist to schedule her next visit. She is moving in slow motion and she is sick to her stomach with disbelief and fear.

Her next appointment made, Andrea takes the stairway down to the parking garage. Having located her Toyota pickup, she unlocks the door, sits behind the wheel, locks the door, and tries to find the ignition with her key. Her tears are coming hard now and she lets her grief take her. The confirmation of her pregnancy is more than she can bear. Her cries of anguish fill the small cab for the next five minutes.

This wasn't supposed to happen. Raised in a Christian family with love and strong moral principles, Andrea knows right from wrong. She knows it was right to date Craig, a fellow believer and business school student. But it was wrong to let a wonderful dinner and glass of wine lead to an act of intimacy reserved for marriage. She had taken precautions, which had obviously failed her. More importantly, she had failed herself and her God.

Starting her cherry-red truck, Andrea dries her face and pulls her blonde hair back into a ponytail and leaves the garage, numb, but determined to make it to her apartment and sort things out. As she drives, she begins to give voice to her feelings.

"I am so sorry, Father; I cannot believe I let this happen. I'm ashamed of myself; I'm scared; I'm mad. I… I want to throw up." Quickly pulling the truck to the curb, Andrea steps out and gets rid of her breakfast. With tears streaming down her face, she climbs back in and cleans up.

"That is a fitting act," she whispers. "That is probably what You think of me, huh? It's what I think of me. How, how, how could I be so stupid?"

In one moment, Andrea's plans for her life now appear as a puzzle dumped out on a table. What will her parents think? Her friends? What will Craig say? *What do I do?* She feels sick again, but keeps driving.

Arriving at her apartment complex, she pulls into her numbered space, runs up the stairs, and into the security of her familiar home. Throwing her keys and purse on the table, Andrea sits on the bed where it all started. Tears come again as she lays down and hugs her pillow. As her sobs subside, she turns toward her one window, where the bouquet of flowers from Craig are in silhouette. She ponders his gift and her feelings for him, now confused. Was it love or lust? Was it to please him or was it my desire?

One of Andrea's favorite things to do in life is to scuba dive. For some reason, she thinks of her last buddy dive during her certification test. The act of sharing one air hose is stuck in her head. It takes her mind from the moment, and she is there, breathing and relying on another person for her life.

Suddenly, it hits her. The child. She has only thought of the life within her as a problem, not as a person. Now she does and instinctively hugs her stomach. This child is sharing her air, her blood, her life. It is relying on her to stay alive. It needs her; it wants to live.

She rolls on to her back and looks at the ceiling, suddenly clear on one issue. "Father, I don't know much about my life right now, and I hope that You will show me. But, I do know this: my mistake has started a life, and I will not end it. I won't fix my mistake with another mistake. Thank you for being my friend and for forgiving me. Help me to forgive myself and to know how to handle all of this. I'm scared, but I'm going to trust You to lead me. I know you won't let me down."

With that said, Andrea closes her eyes and feels embraced by a peace within her heart. She knows many decisions are in her future, but, right now, she just wants to sleep. And so she does.

Pebbles Along My Path

We need daily touches from the Master...

Moments when our eyes are opened to the daily grace we are all given.

The foundational principles of the universe are functioning and true whether we believe in them or not. Unseen power is sustaining and ordering all of the natural world, every moment of every day.

We are all just wind and clay...

...held together, we know not how. We did not rise from the clay bed of earth by our own power; rather, we were raised up by the One who holds all power.

All that we have and all that we are is a gift from Him. We may not understand why we are here, but we can all give thanks for the fact that we are here.

It is so desperately easy to go through our daily lives and never be aware of the awesomeness of just being here, as opposed to being nowhere.

Like sunlight reflecting off the water...

...we can return thanks to the One who gave us life upon this chosen planet in this particular solar system at this exact moment in time. Our goal should be to give thanks for all things and at all times, for we are the recipient of all things.

As a well of deep water…

…our giving of thanks should start with the surface things and then go ever deeper into the hidden rooms of our soul, drawing out those thoughts that dwell within, be they positive or negative, giving Him thanks for everything that makes us who we are. We can go there confidently, once we have learned the way of thanksgiving, because we will not be ashamed of what we will find.

We will come to realize, at a deeper level, that He is already there and knows what it is we shall find there.

Give us this day our daily breath…

…is a prayer that should be uttered by every living creature. We hardly ever consider the fact that breathing air on this wondrous planet is a gift. The very act of breathing keeps us from the condition known as death. To breathe is to know that I am alive. All of my spoken words come from the air I breathe. Therefore, it would be appropriate to give a portion of those words back to the Giver of air in the form of thanks, each and every day.

When one is not thankful, one is blind…

…to just how bad the situation could be, and probably is, for millions of other souls. As we progress on the path that leads us back to the One who made us, our hearts and eyes are opened to the needs and desires of others.

When this begins to happen, thankfulness flows at a much greater pace.

Deep down, in the inner garden of our heart…

…is a yearning to return to the garden of relationship with Him who gives us all things. We sense there was a moment when we rose from the soil of the earth by a power not of our own and we feel again His breath of life in our lungs as we survey His magical creation before the taint of disobedience caused the pillars of perfection to crumble.

We are, all of us, sojourners…

…walking a path through life that is innately known and uniquely ours. When our pathway ends, it shall be continued by no one else. Our DNA and fingerprints verify that which we know in our hearts about our individuality.

It is a wondrous gift to know that I am the only one of me. This knowledge shall empower me to discover and access all of my gifts and abilities as I express my constant thanksgiving to the One who gives me daily life.

If my heart is not filled with thanksgiving…

…it will seek to be filled with the fading treasures of this world and with attitudes that cannot pass through the veil into the presence of the One who made all things. There is no vacuum in the universe; all things are filled with something. We have the privilege and the power to choose that with which we shall be filled.

To be truly thankful in the moment…

…is an exercise in Kingdom living, preparing our hearts for the shedding of these snake skins and the donning of our spiritual wings. Like any exercise, it is at first painful and cumbersome to perform, and we are tempted to give up our new heart habit and return to our slovenly ways.

Soon, though, we begin to sense a change in our handling of life as we become fitter and stronger while our heart grows, we know not how.

The hardest things to be thankful for…

…are those things that bring the most pain and those that we do not understand. And yet, as we look back on the moment or season of trial, we are able to see at least some of the good within it. Hindsight grants us the perspective to see most clearly the things that hurt us the most. Even children can look back on moments of discipline and see that love was the motivation for it.

When I most need sunshine on my face…

…is when I can usually be found hiding in the shadows of my ungrateful heart. It is like a dark alley that I seek to hide in when I have been hurt. To be thankful for the moment is far from my mind as I ponder the possible reasons for this to be happening to me. My heart and my head are cast down; my posture is stooped as I consider lying down on the bed and curling into the fetal position.

Then, like the petal of a flower detecting warmth from above, I turn my face upward, toward the sun, and then I am warmed by the possibilities of the moment, giving thanks for His overseeing Hand.

As those around me speak in tones of negativity…

…I find myself being drawn to the flame as surely as the moth, enjoying the warmth of the camaraderie as we pick at the problems of our workplace and the one who is in authority over us. I fail to ponder and share how grateful I am for the work and the divine stroke of circumstance for me to be where I am at all. I come to my senses, excuse myself and walk away, vowing to change the perspective and direction of the conversation the next time.

As many folks wonder and speculate…

…as to why birds sing so early in the morning, I, myself, believe there is sufficient evidence to suggest they are simply giving thanks and praise to the One who gave them life and song. He says He knows when one of His sparrows falls to the earth, never to fly or sing on earth again. So surely must their songs in the morning give Him great pleasure, knowing they are from the heart and are freely given to the Author of all songs.

The cravings of the human heart has a voice...

...that speaks loud and clear for more of everything, day after day. We feel powerless to silence the voice and are worn out from the struggle to meet the demands. Alas, the way to muffle the noise is to stop and give thanks for what I presently have, allowing the voice of contentment to do battle with the screams of my cravings. It is a battle I am called to win.

In the middle of the night, I arise and step outside...

...into the full moon light, unable to sleep because of that which is troubling my soul. I gaze upward and see Orion, still in formation, while in the East, the planet Venus is making her appearance. I look to the moon and consider its daily pull on the tides of the sea that I have come to love and rely on. I am humbled by the evidence of His consistent care and power for me, every moment of every day and while I sleep in the night.

My troubles fade as I give Him thanks for allowing me to be a part of His most wondrous creation and for the chance to learn and grow as His child.

As a complaint begins to form in my heart...

...seeking expression through my tongue and emotions, I have a flash of thought that tells me this is an opportunity to be thankful and to silence the voice of discontent. At this point, I must decide whether the pleasure I get from complaining is worth the effect on my soul. This habit of thought can be robbed of its power by the giving of thanks. The victory is mine for the taking.

To walk with thanksgiving in my heart...

...unleashes a great power in my life. It is not unlike the lifting of a veil, allowing me to see a bit more of the reality of my existence. Each time I acknowledge my daily blessings, my eyes are opened progressively and my mind is charged with positive thoughts, not only about my Creator, but also about myself.

The very idea of offering up our thanks to Him...

...can seem as unworthy of a gift as if a squirrel were to leave a filbert on the doorstep of the nut farmer from whom he has been stealing his entire life. Now, the farmer would probably have to smile at the thought of the squirrel offering to him that which was his in the first place.

Since we owe our very existence to Him, let us offer up our nut with joy at the thought of Him smiling at our gift with love in His heart for all of us squirrels.

I scoop up a handful of soil...

...and roll it between my fingers. I add a bit of water and ponder how He was able to make my beautiful and complex body from ingredients such as these. Now, I blow my breath across this mud and think about how His breath of Life raised me up from the earth to live and grow in preparation for my walk with Him throughout eternity. I am humbled by His power and creativity.

I am deeply grateful that He considered me enough to put me on His potter's wheel of Life and shape me into who I am today.

To gather in a room around a table...

...with a group of talented and blessed people that are under the illusion that they are self-made and are the chief architect of their successes; to gather with them on the Day set aside to give thanks, and then partake of the feast with virtually no acknowledgement of where it all came from; this is truly a painful and appetite-quenching experience.

As I sit on the sand with a young child...

THE THANKSGIVING HANDBOOK

...we listen to the roar of the crashing surf and the familiar cry of the seagulls above, and we are happy. We dig a hole in the sand and watch it fill with the sea. She flips some sand onto my leg and starts to giggle at her accomplishment. I flip sand on her leg and now we are both laughing in the sheer fun of the moment. As we settle down and get back to the serious task of digging a hole in the sand, I quietly thank Him for the pleasure of being in her company at this moment and in this place. I look into her eyes and see delight and wish for her to have many more moments of simple pleasure as she walks her given path in life.

I sometimes wonder where I was...

...before the magic of conception marked the beginning of my life on this amazing and wondrous planet. We can watch the development and growth of our bodies within our mothers, but where was the *me* that makes up who I am? Where was the spirit and the soul of my personality?

Did the Master dream me up out of His imagination? Was I conscious before I came to earth and I just can't remember any of it? I feel like such a child on this subject, and, I guess I am.

The question of my existence before my birth is probably one of my top three that I look forward to asking Him some day. I hope I will be able to understand the answers that He gives me. Until then, I thank Him for thinking of me and giving me the chance to be able to ponder these things.

I am sitting on a smooth, lichen-covered rock...

...in an alpine meadow, gazing at the snowy peak above me, when I feel a bite on my leg. I instinctively swipe at it and knock an ant back to the soil. I watch him continue on his way to wherever that is. I turn my gaze from the peak above and watch as he and his companions carry items down into their home below the rock upon which I sit.

I ponder their life below and am reminded that there are many worlds within this world. A heavy rain can cause problems in the ant world as real as the problems that I encounter. They must deal with them or perish, just like me.

I lift my gaze again to the peak and whisper my thanks to Him for His loving care and the instincts that He gives to the lowly ant, and to me.

When it comes to the practice of giving thanks...

...we are all as young children, believing that some things are a gift and worthy of thanks, like a present given at Christmas. But, the rest of life is something I make and therefore there is no obvious reason to thank anyone except myself and my hard work.

When the light of understanding comes and my eyes are opened to all that truly is a gift, I go from childhood to maturity in preparation for my place in his wondrous, eternal kingdom.

Thankful Moments Journal

Every day is a miracle, whether we believe it or not. Every day there is a sunrise, whether we see it or not. Every night Orion takes its place across the heavens to be observed or pondered, whether we notice it or not. Every day a flower blooms to feed a bee and show to me the glory of the One who made the flutterby, and me.

There is much to be thankful for, whether we are or not. To come to the feast day in November, the day we have set aside for showing our thanks for all we have and were allowed to experience the past year, to gather with friends and family and not come prepared to share—or not have the chance to share—some moment from the past year can render the day as just another day.

The Thankful Moments Journal is for you to have a place to record the moments that touch you or change you in a manner that makes you want to recall it for yourself, and so you can share it with others on Thanksgiving Day.

Now, it is cool and handy and smart to have a place to write the moments down, and maybe you will for a while. But human nature and history says that just like when we decide to start exercising, we start fast and end quick unless we have a purpose, a reason to make it part of our life schedule.

So, let's lay out three good reasons for recording your thankful moments:

1. To have a meaningful memory to bring to the Thanksgiving gathering, thereby potentially blessing someone gathered there.
2. To assist in opening our hearts and minds to the gifts that are made available to us each and every day, knowing that a thankful person is a humble person, which is a pathway quality leading to other qualities.
3. To aid in the metamorphosis process of becoming a person whom the Father of life can be proud of, so that we can one day "enter into His gates with thanksgiving and into His courts with praise…"

Remember, you are forming a new habit. It will take time to go from thinking about doing to actually doing. Our pattern of thought will tell us, "You will remember this moment; you don't need to write it down." That is an inaccurate thought. You *will* forget; you need to write it down, capturing the valuable thoughts and impressions of the moment.

Have you ever been awakened during the night by a thought or an idea that made you believe you should get up from your warm bed and go write it down? If you did not do it, did you remember it the next day? The odds are that you did not.

People who write songs have learned to keep a pad and pen by their bed so they can record those moments of inspiration. They have learned the hard way that, like the morning dew, it is gone when they awaken. Do not take the chance of trying to recall it later. Do the easy thing: write it down.

References

Leviticus 22:29, "And when you will offer a sacrifice of thanksgiving unto the Lord, offer it at your own (free) will."

1 Chronicles 16:7–36, "Then David delivered first this psalm to thank the Lord…"

1 Chronicles 16:8, "Give thanks unto the Lord, call upon His name, make known His deeds among the people…"

Psalm 92:1, "It is a good thing to give thanks unto the Lord and to sing praises to thy name."

Psalm 97:12, "… give thanks at the remembrance of His holiness."

Psalm 100:4, "Enter into His gates with thanksgiving and into His courts with praise, be thankful unto Him and bless His name."

Psalm 105:2, "Let us come before His presence with thanksgiving…"

Psalm 107:1, "Oh, give thanks unto the Lord, for he is good…"

Psalm 116:17, "I will offer to thee the sacrifice of thanksgiving…"

Psalm 119:62, "At midnight I will rise to give thanks unto Thee because of thy righteous judgments (deeds)…"

Psalm 136:26, "Oh, give thanks unto the God of heaven…"

Daniel 6:10, "Now when Daniel knew that the writing was signed, he kneeled three times a day and prayed and gave thanks."

Matthew 15:36, "Then Jesus took the seven loaves and fishes and gave thanks."

2 Corinthians 9:15, "Thanks be to God for His unspeakable gift."

Ephesians 5:20, "Giving thanks always for all things."

Revelation 11:17, "Blessing and glory and wisdom and thanksgiving... be unto our God..."

1 Timothy 4:3–4, "Receiving God's gifts with thanksgiving sanctifies the gift."

2 Timothy 2:14, "... of these things, put them in remembrance."

To contact Robert visit www.robertcozby.com

www.ingramcontent.com/pod-product-compliance
Lightning Source LLC
LaVergne TN
LVHW012000070526
838202LV00054B/4986